Cover photo: The USS *Iowa*, largest battleship ever built, and the fourth to bear the name, hits the water at the New York Navy Yard in Brooklyn, August 27, after being sponsored by Mrs. Ilo Browne Wallace, wife of the vice president. Note Williamsburg Bridge in background.

AUTHOR
Lawrence Burr

DESIGN
Kelly Oaks

EDITOR
Steve Catalano

PRODUCTION
Brennan Knight

COPY EDITOR
Patricia Bower

CONTENTS

ACKNOWLEDGMENTS

The author wishes to acknowledge the significant help and assistance of the following: David Way, curator, and Mike Getscher, executive vice president and chief operating officer, Battleship *Iowa* Museum, for providing a wealth of ship records, including action reports, war diaries, and details on the turret explosion. Mary Ames Booker, Battleship *North Carolina*, for providing detailed plans of the ship's turret and magazine structure. Captain Greg Kouta (Retired), Memorial Ship *MIKASA*, for recommending our visit to Kure Maritime Museum and the Mutsu gun turret at Etajima. Dr. William Cogar, chief executive of the Historic Naval Ships Association, Annapolis, for providing us with access to his fleet of naval ships and the delights of Annapolis. Finally, to my wife, Judith, for her continued encouragement, research, and naval photographic skills.

The battleship USS *Iowa* (BB-61) takes water over the bow while under way in heavy seas during Operation Ocean Safari '85. (NARA)

The service ribbons earned by the battleship USS *Iowa* during World War II and the Korean War. (NARA)

INTRODUCTION

USS *IOWA* **MARKED THE CULMINATION AND ZENITH** of U.S. battleship development. Her design, construction, armor, armament, motive power, control, and radar technology created a global operational capability that, when manned by U.S. sailors, could not be matched. The firepower of USS *Iowa*'s 9 16-inch/50-caliber and 20 5-inch/38-caliber guns have thundered across the Pacific, Atlantic, Caribbean, Mediterranean, Baltic, and Arctic oceans and seas, firing 14,707 rounds of 16-inch/50 shells in support of freedom and democracy.

Key drivers to the creation and operation of USS *Iowa* were three U.S. presidents, Theodore Roosevelt, Franklin Roosevelt, and Ronald Reagan, who all focused on making and keeping the United States as the strongest naval power on the globe.

The *Iowa* was commissioned on 22 February 1943, after taking 32 months to construct at the Brooklyn Navy Yard. Nearly 2,800 men brought the massive 45,000-ton ship of armored steel to life, as designed from the cumulative experience of its 60 predecessor U.S. battleships and driven by innovative construction and creative American-engineered electric and motive technology.

The strength and quality of her design and construction, coupled with a post–World War II and -Korea enhanced maritime strategy, enabled *Iowa* to be recommissioned and modernized in 1984 with a new suite of computerized communications, radar, nuclear armed missiles, and drones, along with her original main armament of nine 16-inch/50-caliber guns.

The success of the *Iowa* design flowed through to three additional *Iowa*-class battleships, USS *New Jersey* (BB-62), USS *Missouri* (BB-63), and USS *Wisconsin* (BB-64), and these ships served from World War II through Operation Desert Storm in 1992.

Battleship *Iowa* is now the flagship of the new National Museum of the Surface Navy in San Pedro, California. Open to the public, visitors can now appreciate that this magnificent ship is a testimony to the skills of U.S. Navy ship designers, the shipbuilding skills of the Brooklyn Navy Yard, the inventive and technological abilities of U.S. industry, and the professional and heroic skills of the U.S. sailors who stayed on duty against multiple enemies over decades of operational experience.

POST–CIVIL WAR

Following the Civil War, the United States focused on major domestic issues to repair its economy from its wartime financial debt and to develop the agricultural, mineral, and industrial resources that were discovered as a national sense of Manifest Destiny spread across the country. The completion of the transcontinental railroad in 1869 spurred movement west across the continent. Waves of immigrants expanded economic activity. As a result of national energies expended elsewhere, a pause in warship construction ensued, lasting from 1866 to 1883.

Eventually America's burgeoning economic activity itself demanded broader strategic thinking for the U.S. Navy as the country's horizons shifted from coastal defense and commerce raiding to oceanic perspectives. Congress and the American public engaged in a major debate on the military needs of the United States. In 1879, 49 naval engineering officers were, by order of Congress, allocated to colleges and universities throughout the U.S. to establish and teach courses in maritime steam engineering and iron-ship building. A dynamic influence in the debate was *The Naval War of 1812*, written by a young Theodore Roosevelt in 1882. Roosevelt argued that the lack of preparation by the president, Congress, and Navy had undermined the effectiveness of the American military. Roosevelt was drawing parallels between 1812 and the status of the U.S. Navy at that time.

The year 1882 also saw the establishment of the Office of Naval Intelligence, whose critical task was to collect and evaluate industrial, military, and naval intelligence. In 1884 the U.S. Navy established the Naval War College for postgraduate education of officers on the principles and strategy of war. Three new steel cruisers—the USS *Atlanta* (1884), *Boston* (1884), and *Chicago* (1884)—marked the renaissance of the U.S. Navy from the post–Civil War suspension of warship construction.

THE FIRST BATTLESHIPS

A process of design and strategic rethinking led to the first U.S. Navy battleship, the USS *Texas* (1892), and would eventually culminate in the *Iowa*-class battleships. Reflecting reduced American ship-designing capability due to the protracted hiatus in building warships, the Navy Department in August 1886 held a worldwide competition for the design of a steel battleship. The winning bid for the *Texas* was submitted by William G. John, the general manager of Barrow Shipbuilders and formerly of the Admiralty's ship design team in London.

The design clearly reflected the mix of uses envisioned for battleships in the late Victorian era. Two turrets were mounted in echelon, allowing fore and aft firing capability for the single 12-inch gun in each turret. The design also incorporated six torpedo tubes, plus two torpedo boats carried on board. The ram-bow structure completed the offensive equipment.

The U.S. Navy undertook the task of developing its armament capability with the expansion of the Washington Navy Yard in 1886. This focused the need for large gun forgings. For armor, it relied on the American iron and steel industry, which had yet to adequately adapt its steel manufacturing to produce armor plate. A partnership was established by Bethlehem Iron in January 1886, when it reached an agreement with Joseph Whitworth of Manchester, England. Whitworth was a major provider of steel and armor plate to the Royal Navy. The agreement included the patent rights on armor production plus the purchase of a Whitworth Steel plant to be dismantled and shipped from England to the United States. This plant included two hydraulic forging presses of 2,000- and 5,000-ton capacity, a complete fluid-compression forging plant that included a press of 7,000-ton capacity, a 125-ton hydraulic crane, plus lathes and boring mills. Additionally, Bethlehem acquired the designs for open-hearth furnaces and tools and an agreement to exchange engineers. Compared to the Bessemer process, the open-hearth furnaces provided a faster way to increase steel production and more easily harden steel into armor. In June 1887 the Navy entered a contract for Bethlehem to supply 6,700 tons of armor and 1,300 tons of gun forgings to the Navy.

In 1890 the Navy contracted with Carnegie Steel for 6,000 tons of nickel-steel armor from its new Homestead steel plant. Carnegie Steel had also acquired a heavy-forging plant from Whitworth. As a result, the Navy was no longer dependent on just one supplier for its armor needs. However, transferring and reassembling a steel plant in the United States, then perfecting the operational skills to produce armor that would meet the Navy's exacting standards, meant that deliveries of armor to the shipbuilders were long delayed.

Following the USS *Texas*, Congress authorized three coastal defense battleships in June 1890: the USS *Indiana* (BB-1), *Massachusetts* (BB-2), and *Oregon* (BB-3). The *Oregon* was built at the Union Iron Works in San Francisco, which had earlier built the cruisers USS *Charleston* (C-2) and *San Francisco* (C-5) to further underpin shipbuilding capability on the Pacific coast, before the Panama Canal was constructed.

The armament mix for these three battleships called for four 13-inch main guns that were to be supported by a secondary battery of 6-inch rapid-fire guns, as fitted to European battleships. The fact that the U.S. Navy and American industry could not yet manufacture the steel for naval guns meant that these guns had to be imported. Faced with this fact, the Navy chose to mount 8-inch guns, again imported, heavier but slower-firing than 6-inch guns, so that U.S. battleships would be more heavily armed than potential adversaries.

Operating the three coast-defense battleships provided a learning experience for naval ship designers. A lesson in point involved the main gun turrets on board USS *Indiana*. The circular turrets required that guns be mounted near the front face of the turret so they could be elevated. This meant that the turret's center of balance was four feet forward of the turret's y-axis. Therefore, when the turrets were trained over the port or starboard beam, the ship heeled several degrees to that side, making gun laying difficult, straining the turret-turning machinery, and submerging the side armor belt. During a heavy storm in 1896, the gun turrets on board the *Indiana* broke free from their stops and swung from side to side as the ship heeled to the storm-wave motion. It took hundreds of her crew to safely lash the gun turrets down.

For coast-defense operations the ships took on 400 tons of coal, and their freeboard of 12 feet made them wet in a seaway. Seawater entering the main gun turrets put the turret machinery at risk. However, the USS *Oregon* steamed 14,000 miles from San Francisco around South America and northward in the Atlantic to join the U.S. Fleet off Key West, Florida, in May 1898. It then took part in the blockade of Cuba and the Battle of Santiago de Cuba during the Spanish-American War. The first combat experience for the new U.S. battleships occurred with the engagements of the USS *Oregon*, *Texas*, *Indiana*, and *Iowa* in the Battle of Santiago, 3 July 1898.

THE FIRST USS *IOWA* (BB-4)

In July 1892 Congress authorized the construction of a 9,000-ton seagoing coastline battleship meeting the Navy's need for a battleship that could operate in the open waters of the Atlantic and Pacific. The design of this, the first USS *Iowa*, achieved the Navy's objectives with a longer forecastle and a higher deck height above the waterline, which made her a drier ship and decreased maintenance for the forward gun turrets. The *Iowa* also carried 1,795 short tons of coal, a larger volume than her three battleship predecessors.

The *Iowa* carried a heavy armament of four 12-inch guns in two turrets, one fore and one aft. The turrets were a new design, oval in shape. The guns and turrets were balanced properly and kept the ship on an even keel when trained over the beam. *Iowa* also carried eight 8-inch guns in four turrets, two portside and two starboard side. Six 4-inch guns were carried in single sponsons, three aside, with a further 20 6-pounder guns in casements along her main deck. This profusion of guns reflected the growing risk represented by torpedo craft and the need to overwhelm them with rapid-fire guns before they could launch their torpedoes. *Iowa*'s armor was the new Harvey heat-treated armor from open-hearth furnaces.

The most visible feature of USS *Iowa* was her two smokestacks, each 100 feet high. These gave the ship a natural draft and decreased the need to pressurize the firerooms.

Table 1: Key Features of Early Battleships

Class (number of ships)	Displacement (tons)	Speed (knots)	Armament	Armor (belt)	Fuel	Endurance (miles)
Texas (1)	6,315	17	2 × 12-in/35-cal 12 × 6 pdr 6 torpedo tubes	12-in.	Coal	6,000
Indiana (3)	10,225	15.5	4 × 13-in/35-cal 20 × 6 pdr 6 torpedo tubes	18-in.	Coal	5,640
Iowa (1)	11,400	17	4 × 12-in/35-cal 8 × 8-in 6 × 4-in 20 × 6 pdr	14-in.	Coal	5,140

THE PRE-DREADNOUGHTS

Following the authorization of USS *Iowa* and the success of the U.S. Navy in the Spanish-American War, the Treaty of Paris formally ended the war on 10 December 1898. Under the treaty's terms, the United States gained possession of the Philippines, Puerto Rico, and Guam from Spain. Cuba gained its independence from Spain and ceded Guantánamo Bay to the United States. With Puerto Rico and Guantánamo Bay as military bases for the Army and Navy, the United States controlled the entrance and exit to the Caribbean and the future Panama Canal. The United States consolidated its Pacific position with the annexation of Hawai'i on 12 August 1898. In one "splendid little war," as Secretary of State John Hay called it, and with a quiet overthrow of Hawai'i's queen and government, the United States became a major international power.

Following the Spanish-American War, three new battleships were authorized and built between 1896 and 1901. The ships of this new *Illinois* class were armed with 13-inch guns and carried 14 6-inch

Commissioned in 1897, the first USS *Iowa* took part in the Battle of Santiago. (Library of Congress)

On the "Iowa"—Marine Guard Drilling.
Copyright 1899 by Strohmeyer & Wyman...

Schlonley Underwood & Underwood.
New York, London, Toronto Canada, Ottawa Kansas.

no 2.

Marine guard drilling on Battleship USS *Iowa*, 1899. (Library of Congress)

guns housed in individual casemates located equally on both beams.

A major feature of this period was the role of President Theodore Roosevelt, who was committed to establishing the U.S. Navy as a force that would equal the navies of Great Britain, Germany, France, Italy, and Japan. President Roosevelt had sailed on USS *Iowa* when he was Acting Secretary of the Navy, to review gunnery exercises off the Virginia Capes. The 8-inch guns fired first at the target 2,000 yards from USS *Iowa*. Then the 12-inch main guns fired, and the target disappeared, much to Roosevelt's satisfaction.

The Roosevelt name became strongly related with the USS *Iowa* and was far more significant than a volume of 8-inch and 12-inch gunfire. On becoming president, Theodore Roosevelt made the growth and international standing of the U.S. Navy paramount in his priorities. A measure of President Roosevelt's approach can be seen in his standing up to the Kaiser of Germany and to Great Britain over the financial problems they had with Venezuela. Placing the entire U.S. Fleet under the command of Admiral George Dewey and stationing the Fleet in the Caribbean close to the German and Royal Navy ships that were blockading Venezuela quickly brought about a peaceful resolution.

The next class of battleships were the *Maine* class, built from 1899 to 1904. They were armed with 12-inch guns to take advantage of the new smokeless powder. This powder gasified almost completely when fired, and the increasing pressure could accelerate a projectile along a gun of 40 or more calibers in length. The flatter trajectory of the shell translated to more accurate firing at longer ranges. These ships used Niclausse boilers, which proved to be heavy users of coal, thus resulting in lower endurance levels.

Congress approved 21 battleships in the period up to 1907, which were subsequently classed as pre-dreadnoughts. In 1907 President Roosevelt ordered the U.S. Navy to undertake a global voyage with 16 battleships, which was referred to as the Great White Fleet. Under the command of Rear Admiral Robley Evans, who had captained USS *Iowa* to victory at the Battle of Santiago, the Fleet left Hampton Roads on 17 December 1907. The Fleet comprised the following battleships: *Connecticut* (BB-18), *Kansas* (BB-21), *Vermont* (BB-20), *Louisiana* (BB-19), *Georgia* (BB-15), *New Jersey*, *Rhode Island* (BB-17), *Virginia* (BB-13), *Minnesota* (BB-22), *Maine* (BB-10), *Missouri*, *Ohio*, *Alabama* (BB-8), *Illinois* (BB-7), *Kearsarge* (BB-5), and *Kentucky* (BB-6). In support of this Fleet and recognizing the distances and time needed to complete the voyage, six auxiliary ships sailed in support of the Fleet. As the Panama Canal was in the future, the Fleet had to sail through the Straits of Magellan at the southern tip of South America to reach the western coast of the United States. In San Francisco, reached on 6 May 1908, Rear Admiral Evans passed the command of the Fleet over

Table 2: Key Features of Pre-Dreadnought Battleships

Class (number of ships)	Lead Ship Commissioned	Displacement (tons)	Speed (knots)	Armament	Armor (belt)	Fuel	Endurance (miles)
Kearsarge (2)	20 February 1900	11,540	17	4 × 13-in/35-cal 4 × 8-in 14 × 5-in 4 torpedo tubes	16.5	coal	5,070
Illinois (3)	16 September 1901	11,565	17	4 × 13-in/35-cal 14 × 6-in 16 × 6 pdr 4 torpedo tubes	16.5	coal	4,190
Maine (3)	29 December 1902	12,370	18	4 × 12-in/40-cal 16 × 6-in 6 × 3-in 2 torpedo tubes	11	coal	5,660
Virginia (5)	7 May 1902	15,000	19	4 × 12-in/40-cal 8 × 8-in 12 × 6-in 12 × 3-in 4 torpedo tubes	11	coal	4,860
Connecticut (6)	29 September 1906	16,000	19	4 × 12-in/45-cal 8 × 8-in 12 × 7-in 20 × 3-in 4 torpedo tubes	11	coal	6,620
Mississippi (2)	1 February 1908	13,000	17	4 × 12-in/45-cal 8 × 8-in 8 × 7-in 12 × 3-in 2 torpedo tubes	9	coal	5,800

to Rear Admiral Charles S. Sperry. In addition, the *Maine* and *Alabama* left the Fleet and were replaced by *Nebraska* and *Wisconsin*.

After visits to 20 ports, from Australia, Japan, South Asia, the Suez Canal, the Mediterranean, and finally Gibraltar, the Fleet returned to Hampton Roads on 22 February 1909. This Fleet was the only fleet of battleships to sail point to point around the world and was a contrast to the Russian Fleet, which had been defeated by Japan after sailing from the Baltic to the Sea of Japan. It was a clear signal to the other naval powers—Great Britain, France, Germany, and Japan—that the United States was now a major naval power with global capability and commercial trading ambitions.

The pre-dreadnoughts evinced a continuing increase in displacement and won the U.S. Navy's increasing confidence in their overall ship design, as measured by the number of ships ordered in a class. An important factor behind these features was the decision by the Navy Board to reject the concept of coastal battleships. Instead, the board adopted the strategy of meeting and engaging any threat to the United States well away from the country's shores. The successes in the battles of Manila Bay in the Philippines and Santiago in Cuba gave clear demonstration of the efficiency of the U.S. Navy in a global setting. The 8-inch gun had proved to be a strong weapon. Its flat trajectory at the ranges fought during the battles did the majority of the damage to the Spanish ships. One shot from a 13-inch gun on board USS *Oregon* created a massive splash just in front of the fleeing *Cristóbal Colón*, which was warning enough to cause the Spanish cruiser to beach herself rather than face a substantial battering from the *Oregon*.

THE DREADNOUGHT ERA

The dreadnought era commenced in the U.S. Navy well before HMS *Dreadnought* was launched in February 1906. The initial issue being considered was the rationale for arming new battleships with all big guns. The argument was made in an article written by Lieutenant Matt Signor for the March 1902 U.S. Naval Institute *Proceedings* magazine. He suggested that new battleships be armed with 2 turrets, each containing triple 12-inch guns. Professor Philip R. Alger, an expert on naval gunnery, wrote in the June 1902 *Proceedings* that 8 12-inch guns carried in double turrets was a preferred structure. Interestingly, the Navy's Bureau of Construction and Repair put forward a proposal in May 1902 for a battleship to be armed with 12 10-inch guns in 6 twin turrets. This proposal was one version for what became the *Mississippi*-class battleships.

The issue driving these suggestions was to defeat the risk to battleships that torpedoes were coming to represent. The major supposition was that the torpedoes would be launched by opposing battleships during a line-of-battle formation and from a distance at which the secondary battery of the defending battleship would be powerless to stop the torpedoes from being fired. Therefore, increasing the distance between the two lines of battle to beyond 4,000 yards, the likely range of torpedoes at that time, would be a relevant response to the torpedo risk. This in turn would mean that big guns were required to battle opposing battleships at the increased range, whereas the secondary battery of 10-inch, 9-inch, or 8-inch guns would become less relevant.

Evolving naval technology developed the torpedo craft into a very fast ship, capable of escorting battleships during battle and thereby becoming a risk to opposing battleships by launching torpedoes. A defending battleship would need a secondary battery with guns powerful enough to destroy a destroyer and sufficiently quick-firing to train an accurate volume of fire on a rapidly moving target. This suggested a gun that could be reloaded by hand with a powerful punch. A 3-inch gun proved to be the best for this task.

The General Board met at the Naval War College for the Newport summer conference in 1903 and discussed these issues. Particular interest was given to the paper by Lieutenant Commander Homer Clark Poundstone, who proposed a uniform main armament of 11-inch/50-caliber guns. Further work by the Naval War College proposed that a secondary battery of 3-inch guns would suffice to repel torpedo attacks.

In March 1905 Congress authorized two battleships with a maximum displacement of 16,000 tons. In

Table 3: Key Features of Dreadnought Battleships

Class (number of ships)	Lead Ship Commissioned	Displacement (tons)	Speed (knots)	Armament	Armor (belt)	Fuel	Endurance (miles)
South Carolina (2)	1 March 1910	16,000	18.5	8 × 12-in/45-cal 22 x 3-in/50-cal 2 × 3 pdr 2 torpedo tubes	12	coal	6,950
Delaware (2)	4 April 1910	20,380	21	10 × 12-in/45-cal 14 × 5-in/50-cal 2 × 3 pdr 2 torpedo tubes	9	coal	6,000
Florida (2)	15 September 1911	21,825	21	10 × 12-in/45-cal 16 × 5-in/51-cal 4 × 6 pdr 2 torpedo tubes	9	coal	5,776
Wyoming (2)	25 September 1912	26,000	21	12 × 12-in/50-cal 21 × 5-in/51-cal 4 × 3 pdr 2 torpedo tubes	5	coal	8,000
New York (2)	15 May 1914	27,000	21	10 × 14-in/45-cal 21 × 5-in/51-cal 4 × 3 pdr 4 torpedo tubes	10	coal	7,060
Nevada (2)	11 March 1916	27,500	20.5	10 × 14-in/45-cal 21 × 5-in/51-cal 2 × 3-in/50-cal 4 torpedo tubes	13.5	oil	8,000
Pennsylvania (2)	12 June 1916	31,200	21	12 × 14-in/45-cal 22 × 5-in/51-cal 4 × 3-in/23-cal 4 torpedo tubes	13.5	oil	7,552
New Mexico (3)	20 May 1918	32,000	21	12 × 14-in/50-cal 14 × 5-in/51-cal 8 × 3-in/50-cal 2 torpedo tubes	13.5	oil	8,000
Tennessee (2)	3 June 1920	32,300	21	12 × 14-in/50-cal 14 × 5-in/51-cal 4 × 3-in/50-cal 2 torpedo tubes	13.5	oil	8,000
Colorado (4)	30 August 1921	32,600	21	8 × 16-in/45-cal 14 × 5-in/51-cal 4 × 3-in/23-cal 2 torpedo tubes	13.5	oil	8,000
South Dakota (6)	Canceled because of the Washington Naval Treaty and never built	43,200	23	12 × 16-in 16 × 5-in 2 torpedo tubes	13.5	oil	8,000

calculating how to include the sufficient armament and motive power into this limited displacement, Chief Constructor Washington Capps found a workable arrangement consisting of eight 12-inch guns in four superfiring turrets, all located on the ship's center line, with a secondary battery entirely of 3-inch guns. The *South Carolina* class became the first all-big-gun battleship for the U.S. Navy. She was launched on 11 July 1908, two years after HMS *Dreadnought*. The delay in completing *South Carolina* (BB-26) reflected the time needed for industry to produce armor plate plus the increased and competitive demand for steel for bridges and skyscrapers.

By 1921 the U.S. Navy had its 21 new battleships in its fleet. Of these, ten were classic dreadnoughts, from the *South Carolina* class to the *New York* class. The *Nevada* class introduced new features: oil fuel replaced coal, geared turbines replaced reciprocating steam engines, triple-gun turrets supplanted twins for the main armament, and a new "all or nothing" concept was adopted in which enhanced armor was concentrated over magazines, boilers, and engines. Nine battleships were built to these principles in the *Nevada* through the *Tennessee* classes.

The *New Mexico*, *Tennessee*, and *Colorado* classes of battleships were equipped with turboelectric drives to couple turbines running at high speed more efficiently with the ship's propellers, which had to turn more slowly than the turbine. Geared turbines addressed this issue, but General Electric (GE) proposed that the turbines could power an electric generator that in turn could power a motor that would turn the propeller shaft.

The *Colorado* class also introduced the 16-inch/45-caliber gun, Mark 1. The gun had been designed in August 1913, test fired in July 1914, and approved for production in January 1917. The General Board debated whether and when this gun could be included within the design phase of a new battleship. The key issue was the weight of the gun and the impact on the final displacement of the proposed battleship. The 16-inch gun proved to be very successful, firing a 2,110-pound shell out to 34,000 yards.

The *Colorado* class was to be followed by the *South Dakota* class, authorized by Congress on 19 August 1916 as part of President Woodrow Wilson's aim to have a navy second to none. The new class was to comprise six battleships of 43,200-ton displacement, a significant increase over the 32,600-ton displacement of the *Colorado* class. However, the entry of the United States into World War I created significant demand for new destroyers and submarine chasers to protect the convoys of U.S. troop ships from German U-boats while conveying American soldiers to Great Britain and France. This delayed the implementation of Congress's authorization for battleships.

WORLD WAR I

After the United States declared war on Germany in April 1917, six U.S. dreadnoughts served as the Sixth Battle Squadron with the Royal Navy Grand Fleet. These six dreadnoughts—USS *New York* (BB-34), *Texas* (BB-35), *Delaware* (BB-28), *Florida* (BB-30), *Wyoming* (BB-32), and *Arkansas* (BB-33)—were chosen because they were coal powered. Great Britain had immense coal resources but no indigenous oil, which had to be imported from Mexico and Iran. The newer oil-fired U.S. dreadnoughts of the *Nevada* (BB-36) and *Pennsylvania* (BB-38) classes were therefore retained in the United States.

The Sixth Battle Squadron sailed with the Grand Fleet on multiple sweeps through the North Sea. These sweeps were designed to locate and engage the German High Seas Fleet, should it venture out from its harbor into the North Sea. In addition, the American dreadnoughts undertook independent convoy-escort duty from the northern United Kingdom to Norway and back. Each convoy and escort duty was seen as high risk, owing to the possibility of a sudden sortie by the German fleet or their battlecruiser arm to catch and destroy the convoy and their escort. Despite Allied expectations, however, and apart from an occasional venture into the North Sea and rapid return, the German fleet spent the war in harbor.

Instead, the primary encounters of U.S. dreadnoughts with the German navy were with U-boats and their torpedoes from below the sea's surface, and reconnaissance Zeppelins monitoring ship movements from aloft. The 3-inch antiaircraft guns carried by the U.S. dreadnoughts could not reach the high-altitude Zeppelins. However, the U.S. dreadnoughts stood proudly in line with the dreadnoughts of the Grand Fleet to take the surrender of the German High Seas Fleet on 21 November 1918.

World War I ushered in airpower as a potent military arm. The long-range bombing of London and western Germany introduced the potential capabilities of aircraft, leading advocates of airpower to wonder if bombers could also sink battleships. The increasing size and cost of battleships versus the capabilities of much-cheaper bomb-laden aircraft was hotly debated both in the United States and Great Britain.

On 1 November 1920 the U.S. Navy conducted a test off the Virginia Capes to determine whether naval aircraft could sink the old battleship USS *Indiana*. As the bombs used were unarmed, the *Indiana* stayed afloat. Further tests were conducted in 1921, with the Army Air Service commanded by General William "Billy" Mitchell taking part. The first test

on 21 June successfully sank ex-German U-boat *U-117* after hits from 12 bombers. On 29 June the old battleship USS *Iowa*, renamed *Coast Battleship #4*, was the target. The *Iowa* sailed into the naval range as a radio-controlled target. Aircraft crews located her, and Navy planes dropped 80 dummy bombs, but only 2 bombs hit the ship. Tests in July showed greater success. Army bombers sank the ex-German destroyer *G-102* in 19 minutes on 13 July and five days later sank the ex-German cruiser *Frankfurt* with 600-pound bombs.

On 20 July the main test against a battleship took place. Attacking the ex-German dreadnought *Ostfriesland*, the first wave of bombers dropped 1,000-pound bombs, with three hits made, but the deck armor was sufficient to keep the ship afloat. On 21 July the second wave of bombers dropped six 2,000-pound bombs. Three bombs were aimed to explode alongside the ship, using the increased water pressure from the explosion to hammer the hull and displace hull plates. *Ostfriesland* sank shortly later.

THE PEN IS MIGHTIER THAN THE DREADNOUGHT

The pens wielded by the diplomats of the United States, Great Britain, France, Italy, and Japan to sign the Washington Naval Treaty (WNT) on 6 February 1922 destroyed more dreadnoughts than all of the guns, shells, torpedoes, and mines used against them in World War I.

The WNT emerged from the financial and human devastation of World War I. The public and politicians realized that new dreadnought battleships needed to be built, both to replace battle-worn and outdated ships and to project national aspirations to maritime power. For the United States, this meant having a navy second to none, specifically compared with the Royal Navy of Great Britain. In 1919 the Royal Navy had 45 dreadnought battleships and battlecruisers compared to the U.S. Navy's 36.

The cost of building and maintaining the fleets of dreadnoughts was beyond both the financial and war-weary willpower of the public and their purse. Recognizing that an all-out race to naval supremacy was unrealistic, the new administration of President Warren

G. Harding was receptive to the increasing messages from the U.K. government that naval-building programs be addressed in an international conference. Accordingly, on 8 July 1921, U.S. Secretary of State Charles Evans Hughes issued an invitation to the United Kingdom, Japan, France, and Italy to join with the United States in a naval arms-limitation conference in Washington, D.C.

In his opening remarks on 12 November, Hughes proposed that "to limit naval armament, competition in its production must be abandoned." He then identified four principles to be followed:

- All actual or projected capital-shipbuilding programs should be abandoned.

- Further reductions should be made by scrapping certain older ships.

- General regard should be given to the existing strength of the powers concerned.

- Capital-ship tonnage should be used as the measurement of strength for navies and a proportion-

The renamed *Iowa*, now *Coast Battleship # 4*, on Miraflores Lake 10 February 1923, on her way to become a target for the Pacific Fleet. (NARA)

ate allowance for auxiliary combatant craft should be prescribed.

These principles led to the famous ratio of 5:5:3 on the size of the fleets for the United States, United Kingdom, and Japan. The implementation of these principles and ratios meant that the U.S. Navy scrapped or sank 17 dreadnoughts and canceled the construction of 6 *South Dakota*–class dreadnoughts. The Royal Navy scrapped 19 dreadnoughts and canceled 4 new *Lion*-class capital ships. Japan was to scrap 10 pre-dreadnoughts and cancel 7 dreadnoughts under construction.

A key determinant in Hughes's proposals was that no new capital ships were to be built during the coming ten-year period. When new constructions were allowed to resume, the standard displacement for new capital ships was set at 35,000 tons, and main armament was limited to a maximum of 16 inches.

Following Hughes's speech and proposals, intense discussions and deal-making commenced between the three main parties. The key components developed from these discussions were that the United States would complete the building of two *Maryland*-class battleships, the USS *Colorado* (BB-45) and *West Virginia* (BB-48), and scrap two dreadnoughts, the USS *North Dakota* (BB-29) and *Delaware*. Two previously proposed battlecruisers, the USS *Lexington* (CV-2) and *Saratoga* (CV-3), were to be constructed as aircraft carriers. The Royal Navy would build two new battleships, HMS *Nelson* and HMS *Rodney*, at the agreed-upon 35,000-ton displacement and maximum main armament of 16 inches, but it would also scrap four of its oldest dreadnoughts. Japan would retain the dreadnought *Mutsu* with her 16-inch main armament and scrap *Settsu*. This gave the Japanese the opportunity to update *Mutsu*'s gun turrets with the turrets from *Settsu*.

An important element of the WNT that was to have a profound effect on the U.S. Navy in future years was the agreement between the United States, United Kingdom, and Japan regarding the number and defensive armaments of naval bases within the Pacific Ocean. The treaty prohibited the three signatories from constructing new fortifications or naval bases in the Pacific Ocean region. Existing fortifications in Singapore, the Philippines, and Hawai'i could remain. The Versailles Treaty of 1919 had already granted Japan mandated authority over the Marshall, Caroline, and Mariana Islands. These islands would constitute a barrier to the U.S. Navy and its reinforcement of the Philippines in the event of military action between the United States and Japan.

The U.S. Navy needed to dominate both the Atlantic and Pacific Oceans to protect both its East and West Coasts. The Royal Navy needed to be dominant in the North Sea, the Atlantic, the Mediterranean Sea, the Indian Ocean, and the seaways to Australia and New Zealand. However, under the terms of the WNT, the sizes of their respective capital-ship fleets were insufficient for these tasks. Neither the U.S. Navy nor the Royal Navy could dominate any one ocean. In contrast, the Japanese were able to dominate the Western Pacific and range as far as Hawai'i.

The WNT stopped the design and construction of battleships for ten years. It also limited cruisers to maximum displacements of 10,000 tons and a maximum of 8-inches for main armament. The U.S. Navy built 18 cruisers to these limits with the *Pensacola* (CA-24), *Northampton* (CA-26), *Portland* (CA-33), *New Orleans* (CA-32), and *Wichita* (CA-45). Many of the cruisers from these classes of ship held the line in the Pacific after the Pearl Harbor attack. They supported aircraft carriers in their raids on the Japanese mandate islands and then defended the Marines on Guadalcanal.

MODERNIZATION

The WNT allowed battleship reconstruction "for the purpose of providing means of defense against air and submarine attack," but reconstruction was not to increase displacement by more than 3,000 tons.

The U.S. Navy had 13 battleships that could be reconstructed in accordance with the WNT. Six of these battleships were coal-fired. As a result of the cancellation of the six *South Dakota*–class battleships, new and unused oil-fired boilers were available to be fitted to these ships.

The dreadnoughts USS *Florida, Utah* (BB-31), *Wyoming, Arkansas, New York,* and *Texas* all received new oil-fired boilers, which increased their cruising range by wide margins. The new boilers did not require as much internal space as the old coal-fired boilers. Ship designers allocated the newly available space to rooms for fire control, crew habitation, and fuel-oil storage. The new boilers also required only a single funnel, instead of two, freeing up deck space for a new fire-control mast structure.

Additional armor was worked into all 13 of the battleships. The primary areas for this work were the turret and conning-tower roofs as well as the decks over magazines, engines, and boiler rooms. The steering-mechanism room, situated aft, also received additional armor protection.

The blisters for torpedo protection provided space for additional fuel-oil storage and provided extra space for the construction of a torpedo bulkhead between the external hull and the engine and boiler rooms. The internal space created by the blister provided space either filled with liquid or left empty to absorb exploding gases before they reached the ship's hull.

A significant addition to all 13 battleships was an aircraft catapult to launch an aircraft for spotting the ship's gunfire. As gun range increased, spotting the fall of shot from the spotting top became increasingly difficult. Firing exercises in 1935 demonstrated that, at ranges over 25,000 yards, aircraft-spotting was six times more accurate than ship-based spotting.

Because of insufficient deck space, the six originally coal-fired dreadnoughts—USS *Florida, Utah, Wyoming, Arkansas, New York,* and *Texas*—had their catapults fitted atop gun turrets. The oil-fired battleships—USS *Nevada, Oklahoma* (BB-37), *Pennsylvania, Arizona* (BB-39), *New Mexico* (BB-40), *Mississippi* (BB-41), and *Idaho* (BB-42)—had sufficient deck space to locate their catapults on their quarterdecks. The catapult was powered by a 5-inch powder bag that could accelerate the ship's aircraft to a flying speed of 55 mph within the 60-foot length of the catapult. The first ship to install the aircraft catapult was USS *Maryland* (BB-46) in May 1922, shortly after her commission into the Navy.

FIRE CONTROL

The WNT's elimination of new battleships channeled warship design into modifying existing battleships through more effective and efficient fire-control operation, which added only minimal weight to the ship's displacement. The addition of an aircraft for spotting was an important element in modernizing the fire-control component of the ship's main armament. USS *Texas* was the first U.S. dreadnought to launch an aircraft in March 1919, when Lieutenant Commander Edward McDonnell piloted a Sopwith Camel from a 20-foot wooden ramp built over her No. 2 superfiring turret while anchored off Guantánamo Bay. The aircraft flew to a landing strip on shore, as there was no means to recover the aircraft on board the *Texas*. Beyond the trial of launching the aircraft, the Sopwith Camel also took part in gunnery exercises by spotting the fall of 14-inch shells fired by *Texas*.

The other elements of modernizing fire control were structured around the Ford rangekeeper. Hannibal Ford had left Sperry Gyroscope in 1914 to establish his own company for designing and manufacturing fire-control equipment. The Ford rangekeeper was originally installed on USS *Texas* in July 1916 when Ford brought a prototype model on board and demonstrated its workings to a group of gunnery officers. The Ford rangekeeper stood on a pedestal attached to the deck. Its glass face covered a series of dials that were turned by numerous handles on the sides of the box.

The Ford rangekeeper was the latest technical attempt at providing a disciplined, reliable, and measurable means to address the fundamental fire-control gunnery questions of where to point the guns and at what range to fire them to hit the target. As such, it constituted a significant advance on the Dumaresq and Dreyer fire-control systems used by the Royal Navy.

A key aspect of fire control was the problem of synchronizing the firing of all the guns at or near the same time. To solve the synchronization problem, the Navy turned to GE, which drew upon the electrical design and equipment they had created to operate the locks and water levels of the new Panama Canal. The electrical equipment built to operate the massive doors of the locks had to work to precise synchronized timing, and had to be seen working from a distant command-and-control room by way of position indicators that replicated the movement of the lock's doors. GE had already supplied electric motors to the Navy for ammunition hoists and a multitude of other tasks requiring power.

Working with Lieutenant William Furlong, the Navy's chief fire-control expert, GE devised automatic procedures to replace follow-the-pointer systems, thereby eliminating human error in pointing the guns. Ships had been relying on inputs from multiple directors, gun turrets, conning towers, and spotting tops. The Navy needed a system that would take those many electric signals for the rangekeeper and convert them to higher power to turn the gun turrets. GE supplied power drives to turn the turrets and designed a switchboard for the plotting room that routed the many electric signals between the gunnery elements. Furthermore, the main gun battery could now be split to engage two targets at the same time, which was an important function for those battleships with two directors.

Prior to 1929 it had been the responsibility of the spotting-top staff to follow the horizon and the heel and yaw of the ship. In that year, however, the U.S. Navy introduced the stable element, a gyroscope that maintained the horizontal and vertical reference points in the plotting room. Located next to the rangekeeper, the stable element also automated the firing of the main guns by waiting for the ship to become level once an officer had already pulled the gun triggers.

The increasing mathematical sophistication of the rangekeeper led to its development into torpedo-data computers for submarines, cruisers, and destroyers. By the early 1930s, the Mark 8 version of the rangekeeper included input for temperature, wind direction and speed, gun wear, and the Earth's rotation.

The mathematical sophistication of the rangekeeper and the successful results of General Mitchell's 1921 bombing tests against a battleship led the U.S. Navy to request Ford Instrument to produce a rangekeeper for antiaircraft defense. The first antiaircraft rangekeeper was produced in 1926. It was a highly complex system that included a variable for the altitude of aircraft to allow a barrage defense against air attacks. During the 1930s, aircraft capabilities and tactics continued to evolve, including high- and medium-level bombing, dive-bombing, torpedo attack, and strafing. The antiaircraft rangekeeper developed along with these air war tactics so that by 1940 it could track targets moving at speeds up to 400 knots in level flight and at 250 knots when diving. As the war progressed and the speeds of attacking aircraft increased, the rangekeeper spread the required calculations between the gun director, the plotting room, and the 5-inch/38-caliber gun mounts.

SUNSET CLAUSE

The WNT had a sunset clause of 31 December 1931. To anticipate the new battleships that would be ordered at the expiration of the WNT, Navy ship designers needed a head start of several years for obtaining requisite design and budgetary approvals. However, the financial overhang from World War I still negatively impacted government budgets, especially in the United Kingdom. An additional issue for the Royal Navy in

1927–1928 was the fast-approaching need to replace the surviving post-WNT dreadnoughts, which had seen heavy war and postwar service.

A conference in Geneva in June 1920 was intended to update the WNT and address the allowable numbers and sizes of cruisers. However, the Geneva Conference was a failure, and the unresolved issues rolled forward to the London Naval Conference of 1930. That conference set certain limits for submarines and light and heavy cruisers but made no changes to the WNT battleship restrictions. In December 1935 a second London Naval Treaty (LNT) was held with the continuing objective of limiting growth in naval armaments. However, changes in the international environment by then caused both Japan and Italy to withdraw from the agreement. Japan's withdrawal would be effective in December 1936.

The remaining parties—the United States, Great Britain, and France—agreed to continue the displacement limits for any new battleships at 35,000 tons and reduced the maximum caliber of battleship guns from 16 inches to 14 inches. A crucial escalator clause was inserted into the agreement: if any of the original signatories to the WNT failed to sign the new LNT before it came into effect on 1 April 1937, the gun-caliber limit would revert to 16 inches. Ultimately, the WNT, the Geneva Accords, and the two LNTs were mooted by the outbreak of war in Europe in September 1939.

Table 4: Treaty Battleships under the WNT

Country	Ship Name	Year Ordered	Date Commissioned	Displacement (tons)	Armaments	Speed (knots)
Great Britain	*Nelson*	1922	August 1927	34,000	9 × 16-in/45-cal 12 × 6-in/50-cal 6 × single 4.7-in 2 torpedo tubes	23
Great Britain	*Rodney*	1922	November 1927	34,000	9 × 16-in/45-cal 12 × 6-in/50-cal 6 × single 4.7-in 2 torpedo tubes	23
France	*Dunkerque*	1931	April 1937	26,500	8 × 13-in 16 × 5.1-in 8 × single 1.5-in	29.5
France	*Strasbourg*	1934	December 1938	26,500	8 × 13-in 16 × 5.1-in 8 × single 1.5-in	29.5
France	*Richelieu*	1935	June 1940	37,250	8 × 15-in 9 × 6-in 12 × 3.9-in 12 × 1.46-in	32
France	*Jean Bart*	1935	December 1940	37,250	8 × 15-in 9 × 6-in 12 × 3.9-in 12 × 1.46-in	32
Italy	*Vittorio Veneto*	1934	April 1940	40,724	9 × 15-in 12 × 6-in 4 × 4.7-in 12 × 3.5-in 20 × 1.5-in	30
Great Britain	*King George V*	1936	December 1940	42,245	10 × 14-in 16 × 5.25-in 64 × 40-mm 10 × 40-mm Bofor	28.3

Table 4 cont.

Great Britain	*Prince of Wales*	1936	March 1941	42,245	10 × 14-in 16 × 5.25-in 64 × 40-mm 10 × 40-mm Bofor	28.3
Great Britain	*Duke of York*	1937	November 1941	42,245	10 × 14-in 16 × 5.25-in 64 × 40-mm 10 × 40-mm Bofor	28.3
Great Britain	*Howe*	1937	August 1942	42,245	10 × 14-in 16 × 5.25-in 64 × 40-mm 10 × 40-mm Bofor	28.3
Great Britain	*Anson*	1937	June 1942	42,245	10 × 14-in 16 × 5.25-in 64 × 40-mm 10 × 40-mm Bofor	28.3
United States	*North Carolina*	1937	April 1941	35,000	9 × 16-in 20 × 5-in 16 × 1.1-in	28
United States	*Washington*	1937	May 941	35,000	9 × 16-in 20 × 5-in 16 × 1.1-in	28
United States	*South Dakota*	1938	March 1942	37,970	9 × 16-in 16 × 5-in 28 × 40-mm	28
United States	*Indiana*	1938	April 1942	37,970	9 × 16-in 20 × 5-in 28 × 40-mm	28
United States	*Massachusetts*	1938	May 1942	37,970	9 × 16-in 20 × 5-in 28 × 40-mm	28
United States	*Alabama*	1938	August 1942	37,970	9 × 16-in 20 × 5-in 28 × 40-mm	28

GERMAN NAVAL REARMAMENT

Germany was not invited to participate in the WNT as it was no longer a naval power. The German High Seas Fleet had surrendered in 1918 and then scuttled itself in Scapa Flow in 1919. Those ships that survived were distributed among the Allies and used as targets. Germany was governed by the Versailles Treaty of 1919, which limited any new battleship construction to 20 years from the launch of the *Braunschweig* class of pre-dreadnought corvettes in 1901. In addition, new construction of naval vessels was limited to a maximum of 10,000 tons.

In 1928 Germany embarked upon a program of building "armor-clad" ships of 10,000 tons and armed with six 11-inch guns in two turrets. The guns were based on the design of the guns carried by German battlecruisers of the High Seas Fleet. Three armor-clad ships were commissioned and earned the name "pocket battleships." These ships followed the terms of the WNT even though Germany was not a signatory to the treaty. In 1935 Adolf Hitler repudiated the Versailles Treaty and entered negotiations with Great Britain on the size of the German navy relative to the Royal Navy. The resulting Anglo-German Naval Agreement lasted until 1939.

Germany also ordered five heavy cruisers of the *Admiral Hipper* class, but only three were actually built. These three ships were larger than the heavy cruisers built by the United States and Great Britain, which firmly adhered to WNT guidelines of 10,000 tons. The *Admiral Hipper* class displaced just over 16,000 tons and carried eight 8-inch guns.

Table 5: German Naval Rearmament

Ship Name	Year Ordered	Date Commissioned	Displacement (tons)	Armaments	Speed (knots)
Deutschland (Renamed *Lutzow*)	1928	April 1933	10,000	9 × 11-in 8 × 5.9-in	28.5
Admiral Scheer	1931	November 1934	10,000	9 × 11-in 8 × 5.9-in	28.5
Admiral Graf Spee	1932	January 1936	10,000	9 × 11-in 8 × 5.9-in	28.5
Scharnhorst	1934	January 1938	31,850	9 × 11-in 12 × 5.9-in 14 × 4.1-in 36 × 1.5-in	32
Gneisenau	1934	May 1938	31,850	9 × 11-in 12 × 5.9-in 14 × 4.1-in 36 × 1.5-in	32
Hipper	1935	April 191939	16,000	8 × 8-in 12 × 4.1-in	32
Bismarck	1935	August 1940	41,700	8 × 15-in 12 × 5.9-in 16 × 4.1-in 16 × 1.5-in	29

PRESIDENT ROOSEVELT AND THE NAVY

The election of Franklin Roosevelt as president of the United States in November 1932 represented a sea change for the growth of the U.S. Navy. Presidential policies and congressional involvement had prevented the U.S. Navy from building its Fleet up to the tonnage allowed by the WNT. The United States was short 150,000 tons of naval construction. As important, the lack of building activity had thrown a large number of shipbuilders out of work and had inhibited the development of armor production. While the United States had not built to WNT tonnage limits, Japan had. By 1936 Japan had reached nearly 80 percent of

parity with the U.S. Navy as measured by tonnage in all categories except battleships.

In 1934 the Vinson-Trammell Act authorized the construction of 102 naval ships over an eight-year period to bring the U.S. Navy up to WNT limits. The Navy commenced construction of destroyers, cruisers, submarines, and auxiliary vessels, along with two aircraft carriers. The same year, President Roosevelt directed the Navy to consider the development of new types of warships if the WNT restrictions were removed within a few years. By May 1935 design lead times were such that the U.S. Navy had to formally call for

A large model of USS *Iowa*'s possible dueling partner, the battleship *Yamato*. Model is in Kure Maritime Museum. (Judi Burr)

design studies for battleships in case the London Naval Conference later that year did not extend the WNT battleship holiday.

As the international environment deteriorated due to German rearmament, Japanese aggression in China, and Italian forays into Africa, President Roosevelt and Congress authorized significant construction additions to the U.S. Navy. The Congressional Appropriation Act for 1937 provided preliminary plans for two new battleships. Construction on them began the following year.

In developing the criteria for the design of the first battleships since the *South Dakota* class of 1921, the designers had to fit their requirements into the WNT displacement limit of 35,000 tons. Over the period 1921–1937, the U.S. Navy moved its strategic focus from Europe and the Atlantic to Japan and the Pacific. The Treaty of Versailles had assigned Japan a mandate over the Marshall, Caroline, and Mariana Islands. Protecting the Philippines would require the U.S. Navy to cross the Pacific and fight through the Japanese-controlled islands. The United States had no naval bases in the Central Pacific, but its modernization programs during the 1920s and 1930s had achieved the strategic imperative of battleships capable of steaming from California to the Philippines.

Fortunately, during the battleship-building hiatus, technological progress in machining and metallurgy contributed to the development of double-reduction geared turbines that weighed less than earlier turbines and without any loss of ship speed. The new turbines also required less internal space than the previous turboelectric-drive machinery, thereby providing additional habitation space for the crew, storage space for fuel, and space for defensive structures.

An important issue was the main gun caliber, which translated into weight and volume dimensions impacting total ship displacement. WNT discussions with the

Mutsu 16-in gun turret. This turret was removed from *Mutsu* and replaced by a turret from *Settsu* as part of the modernization program. The turret is located at Etajima. (Judi Burr)

Inside *Mutsu* 16-in gun turret at Etajima. The *Mutsu* was another potential adversary for the *Iowa*. (Judi Burr)

Royal Navy had considered 12-inch and 14-inch guns as the main armament for any new battleship. However, the cancellation of the U.S. *South Dakota* class had left a large stock of 16-inch guns in storage. The U.S. Navy had equipped five classes of dreadnoughts with 14-inch guns and standardized 16-inch/45-caliber guns as the main armament of the new *Colorado* class of battleships. That decision was a response to the superior range of the Royal Navy's *Queen Elizabeth* class, with their battle-proven 15-inch guns, and the *Nelson* class, with their 16-inch guns. In addition, the Japanese *Nagato* class of two battleships, with 16-inch guns, needed to be considered, together with the lack of information on Japanese naval plans both for modernization of existing battleships and new battleship construction.

The Naval War College employed war games to test strategic thinking across a range of potential naval adversaries. Annual "Fleet problems" exercises of the Fleet at sea explored both the strategic and tactical issues of fleet management and maneuver. The Naval War College, as part of its course, posed problems to the class of commanders on how they would deal with the issues of a transpacific voyage. They would be faced with the continuing threat and action by submarines, aircraft from island airfields, aircraft carriers, and fast Japanese battleships.

A key question was the optimum structure for the Fleet's sailing formation. Significant study had been made of the Royal Navy's Admiral John Jellicoe's Grand Fleet box formation of five columns each with four battleships as he sailed across the North Sea to battle the German High Seas Fleet. The deployment of Admiral Jellico's battleships into a single line of battle took more than 20 minutes to complete. The deployment placed the battleships across the heading of the High Seas Fleet, in the classic "crossing the T" maneuver. It was clear to the commanders that such a rigid box formation was unwieldy when sailing through the mandated islands of the Central Pacific. Commander R. MacFall suggested a circular formation with the flagship positioned in the center. This formation structure would allow a change in direction without the potential for confusion as ships sought their proper station.

Commander Chester Nimitz was part of the group at the Naval War College with Commander MacFall and, when posted to the U.S. Battle Fleet, under the command of Admiral S. Robison, tried the circular formation including the aircraft carrier USS *Langley* (CV-1). The circular formation was sufficiently flexible to allow the Fleet to maintain its relative position to USS *Langley* as she changed course to fly and/or land carrier aircraft.

The need to operate the Fleet over the vast distances of the Pacific Ocean, without access to a naval base west of Pearl Harbor, provided the strategic rationale to build mobile bases that would follow the Fleet. These mobile bases needed to be deployable and capable of repairing damage to a ship's hull as well as to above-water decks and superstructure. This required a mobile floating dry-dock that could lift warships out of the water for access to the hull, rudder, and propellers and shaft. The interwar focus on logistics and the mobile base strategy enabled the Navy to establish the first mobile base at Espiritu Santo in support of the Guadalcanal campaign. In turn, an advanced base sectional dock built in ten sections and rated to hold a 90,000-ton load was built and employed in the Pacific war.

The Navy also focused on developing an air arm, with aircraft carriers as mobile airfields providing air cover for the Pacific Fleet. The U.S. Marines developed an amphibious doctrine and capability to invade and hold Pacific islands. A logistical fleet train capability was also developed to refuel, supply, and repair warships during the cross-Pacific advance.

Table 6: Japanese Battleships

Class (number of ships)	Lead Ship Commissioned	Displacement (tons)	Speed (knots)	Armament	Armor (main belt inches)	Fuel
Fuso (2)	8 November 1915	39,154	22.5	12 × 14-in	12	Oil
Ise (2)	15 December 1917	42,000	23	12 × 14-in	12	Oil
Nagato (2)	25 November 1920	45,950	26.5	8 × 16-in	12	Oil
Kongo (4)	16 August 1913	37,000	35.1	8 × 14-in	8	Oil
Yamato (2)	16 December 1941	61,331	27	9 × 18.1-in	17	Oil

NEW BATTLESHIP DESIGN

All the preparation and design work for the new battleships came to fruition with the USS *North Carolina* (BB-55) being laid down at the Brooklyn Navy Yard on 27 October 1937. Originally designed with a main armament of 14-inch guns in accordance with the WNT and the LNT. The U.S. Navy in July 1937 invoked the escalator clause in the LNT to increase the caliber of the main armament from 14-inches to 16-inches/45-caliber.

In balancing the need for speed with armor protection, main and secondary armament, and the ability to pass through the Panama Canal, the *North Carolina* class of battleships, USS *North Carolina* and *Washington* (BB-56), were subsequently viewed as unbalanced and too slow. The armor's defensive capability against 14-inch shells did not match the ships' offensive capability of 16-inch guns. While fitted with the latest technology of high-pressure boilers and double-reduction turbines, these battleships could not fully keep up with the fleet's aircraft carriers. However, the secondary battery of 20 5-inch/38-caliber dual-purpose guns enabled these ships to provide a significant antiaircraft barrier for themselves and aircraft carriers when they were able to steam near each other.

During the voyage of USS *North Carolina* from the U.S. East Coast to Pearl Harbor, Lieutenant Commander Charles Kirkpatrick developed a manual for air defense that controlled and coordinated Sky Control with the role of radar, directors, and the plot for multiple targets. As the speed of attacking aircraft would be high, the manual set out how to manage the dead time between extracting the shell from the fusing pot, where the shell's fuse was set by the fire-control computer and loading it into the 5-inch gun. A loading delay of more than two seconds would cause the shell to explode after the aircraft had passed the detonation point. The proximity fuzed shells, introduced in 1943 during the Gilbert Islands campaign, negated this issue. The air-defense manual was distributed to the other fast battleships as they arrived in the Pacific.

The subsequent air battle experience of the *North Carolina*– and *South Dakota*–class battleships reinforced the importance of defensive armaments and control and operating systems to be included in the next class of battleships.

During the Battle of the Eastern Solomons on 24 August 1942, the USS *North Carolina* was stationed initially 2,500 yards astern of USS *Enterprise* (CV-6) and was able to project a heavy antiaircraft barrier of bursting 5-inch shells over her while they were steaming at 27 knots. This battle and the role of the *North Carolina* in protecting the *Enterprise* established the role for all the new fast battleships as escorts for the aircraft carriers when they became available in the Pacific.

The *South Dakota* class, including *Indiana* (BB-58), *Massachusetts* (BB-59), and *Alabama* (BB-60), was the next class of fast battleships to be built and commissioned during 1942. The *South Dakota* class was designed to rectify the perceived deficiencies of the *North Carolina* class in that their armor protection was increased to withstand 16-inch shells. The main belt was inclined at 19 degrees, rather than the 15 degrees of the *North Carolina* class. Deck armor was 8.175 inches thick rather than 7.07 inches. This class of battleships was 48 feet shorter than the *North Carolina* class as the designers fashioned the heavier armor into the 35,000-displacement limit imposed both by the WNT and a prewar Congress. The shorter hull also required a more compact engineering and boiler room configuration that resulted in only one funnel being needed. The compact bridge, gun director tower, and funnel fared into the ship's superstructure gave the class a powerful profile but also resulted in a clear aiming point for the enemy, as the USS *South Dakota* (BB-57) was to experience in November 1942.

USS *South Dakota* entered the Pacific in August 1942 and was equipped with 4 mounts of quadruple 40 mm Bofor guns and 36 20-mm Oerlikon antiaircraft guns for close-in defense.

On 26 October 1942, *South Dakota* participated in the Battle of Santa Cruz Islands, defending the USS *Enterprise* against an onslaught of Japanese carrier aircraft. The U.S. aircraft carrier USS *Hornet* (CV-8) was sunk in this battle. The lack of an accompanying fast battleship providing intense antiaircraft fire support to USS *Hornet* was a factor. After the USS *Hornet* was badly hit, the focus for the Japanese aircraft became USS *Enterprise*, attacking her with a wave of 20 dive bombers. USS *South Dakota* was stationed 1,000 yards off *Enterprise*'s starboard side and her firepower added to that of the aircraft carrier and other defending cruisers and destroyers enabled the *Enterprise* to survive. A second wave of torpedo and dive bombers was also repulsed, and in these attacks, the new 20-mm Oerlikon antiaircraft guns proved their worth against low-flying aircraft, along with the new, young crew of *South Dakota* who manned them. *South Dakota* claimed to have shot down over 20 Japanese aircraft during the battle. What is known is that of the Japanese carrier aircrews, 148 did not survive the battle.

The classic role of the battleship in line-of-battle against enemy battleships was still relevant in November 1942, when USS *Washington* and the USS *South Dakota* took on a Japanese bombardment force of the Japanese battleship, *Kirishima*, four cruisers and nine destroyers on the night of 14 November. *Washington*, under the command of Admiral Willis Augustus Lee, leading *South Dakota* and accompanied by four destroyers who were scouting ahead, encountered the Japanese force around Savo Island as it was heading south to bombard Henderson Field and the Marines on Guadalcanal. The four U.S. destroyers were rapidly hit, with two sunk and two on fire. *Washington* steered around the burning destroyers, keeping them between herself and the enemy, while *South Dakota* steered so the burning destroyers were off her port beam silhouetting her against the illumination of the flames and providing a visual target for the Japanese who were to her starboard. The Japanese used their searchlights to illuminate the bridge and tower of *South Dakota*, and in a few minutes the Japanese ships registered 26 hits in a hail of fire on *South Dakota*. The command-and-control features of *South Dakota* were put out of action, but the integrity of the ship was not compromised; however, she was ineffective as a fighting unit and withdrew from the battle, leaving *Washington* alone to fight the Japanese navy.

Fortunately for *Washington*, she had on board two officers who were experts on radar-directed fire control: Admiral Lee and Lieutenant Commander Edwin Hooper. Hooper, who had graduated from both the Naval Academy and MIT, had helped develop, working with industry, fire control as a science and mathematical process and developed the servomechanisms necessary to control and guide the massive gun turrets onto the target. Hooper had joined *Washington* in 1940, just as the ship was fitted with the first main battery fire-control radar sets. Hooper used his experience of working with industry to develop on board *Washington* a servo that allowed the rangekeeper to automatically drive the radar antenna as it tracked the target.

At 0100 on 15 November, *Washington* opened fire on *Kirishima* using her radar to determine location and range. The two battleships were steaming nearly on opposite courses, at first 8,400 yards apart with a combined passing speed of 54 knots. During the battle the range from *Washington* to *Kirishima* opened to 12,650 yards. This meant for *Washington* that her three 16-inch gun turrets were training 20 degrees per minute from 008 degrees to 148 degrees, driven by her radar and rangekeeper.

Fire-control management during the battle was as follows:

- Forward main battery director-controlled fire.
- The stable-vertical director, located in the plotting room controlled continuous level and cross-level.
- Plotting room controlled the firing circuit.
- Radar established range and bearing.

When the forward 16-inch gun turrets hit their stops at 0107, *Washington* ceased fire and had registered nine 16-inch hits from 75 rounds fired. *Kirishima* sank several hours later from the damage she suffered from *Washington*, which was thought to include multiple near-misses of 16-inch shells that may have struck *Kirishima*'s underwater hull.

FAST BATTLESHIP DESIGN

In considering strategic requirements and basic ship characteristics for the next class of battleships, the Navy's General Board saw the need for four fast battleships. In the event of confrontation with Japan, its Pacific strategy under War Plan Orange posited a fleet advance through the Central Pacific to the Japanese-controlled Marshall, Caroline, and Marianas Islands. There the U.S. ships would be exposed to attacks by Japanese fast battleships of the *Kongo* class, armed with 14-inch guns and accompanied by cruisers and destroyers. Japan's two *Nagato*-class superdreadnoughts were armed with eight 16-inch guns. In addition, the U.S. Fleet would be exposed to air attacks from Japanese aircraft stationed either on island airfields or seagoing carriers.

Such a hostile environment required that the U.S. Fleet be accompanied by aircraft carriers to provide defense against air attack. Aircraft carriers required the ability to steam at 30 knots or more to create sufficient airflow over the deck to lift carrier-based aircraft. The carriers themselves needed accompanying warships to protect them from enemy warships and aircraft.

The U.S. Navy would need to counter battleships of the *Kongo* and *Nagato* classes, which were thought to be capable of 26 knots. (The U.S. Navy did not learn until after World War II that a second modernization of the *Kongo* class in 1937 gave these ships a top speed over 30 knots.) The U.S. Navy would also be up against the battleships *Yamato* and *Musashi* but lacked knowledge of their sizes and characteristics.

Admiral Joseph Mason Reeves had led and crafted U.S. carrier airpower. As commander-in-chief of the U.S. Fleet, he brought practical knowledge and the experience of fleet command to his appointment to the General Board in late 1936, where he argued persuasively for fast battleships that could keep up with aircraft carriers.

A target speed of 33 knots was set for the new fast battleships. The General Board agreed that the faster speed would provide flexibility for the ships to be used for special purposes, including leading task forces ahead of the main battle fleet. Their higher speed would enable the new class of fast battleships to accompany aircraft carriers as proposed by Admiral Reeves, creating a powerful task force of mutually supporting fighting ships.

Earlier design studies had suggested that an additional 10,000 tons of displacement for the *North Carolina* and *South Dakota* classes would provide them with the speed to match the aircraft carriers while carrying a heavy main armament. In March 1938, the United States, Great Britain, and France invoked the escalator clause in the LNT to increase the displacement clause to 45,000 tons. Their common interest in escalation was spurred by the rapidly deteriorating European political environment amid German political aspirations and rearmament. In addition to its Pacific concerns, the United States also needed to consider an Atlantic strategy, given that the

German battleships *Bismarck* and *Tirpitz* were under construction, and the battlecruisers *Scharnhorst* and *Gneisenau* were already operational. Italy also had four battleships of the *Littorio* class under construction.

U.S. ship designers agreed that the armor protection for the *South Dakota* class of battleships was acceptable as a basis for the larger fast battleships. The General Board then turned to the issue of the caliber of the main armament. The ships of both the *North Carolina* and *South Dakota* classes were built with 16-inch/45-caliber main armament. However, a 45,000-ton displacement could carry a heavier and more powerful gun. Ordnance trials conducted in 1926 determined that a 16-inch/50-caliber gun could fire a shell at a lower velocity but with greater penetrative power over a longer range. The WNT displacement limits during the late 1920s and early 1930s had eliminated the need to produce such a gun, and the studies were filed for future reference. Now, however, the heavier gun was selected for the new fast battleships. The designers incorporated the gun, gunhouse, supporting barbette structure, and turret into the ship plans.

In June 1939 the ordnance team had produced a new heavy shell for the 16-inch/45-caliber and the new 16-inch/50-caliber guns. The heavy shells were designed to be used in long-range gun actions against battleships and were to be fired at relatively low muzzle velocities and high gun elevations. These conditions would result in a steeper angle of fall, which enhanced the deck-armor penetration capabilities of the shells. The new shells each weighed 2,700 pounds, so the shell-handling system for the big guns was redesigned to use the "super-heavy" armor-piercing Mark 8 shell even before any of the forthcoming *Iowa*-class battleships were laid down.

The focus on the Pacific meant that the new fast battleships had to be designed to pass through the various locks of the Panama Canal. To do so, their beams could not exceed 108 feet. Accordingly, the design of the new fast battleships called for a beam of 108 feet and a length of at least 880 feet, with a displacement of 45,000 tons and a draft of 33 feet. The speed of 33 knots required 230,000 shaft horsepower, produced by eight boilers that drove four sets of geared turbines. This machinery would be positioned amidships, where the greatest space was available for the machinery. This in turn led to the long forward hull shape with a clipper bow, beneath which was a pronounced bulbous bow. The stern featured a twin-skeg structure to provide a clear flow of water to the four propellers and the twin rudders.

USS *Iowa* (BB-61) in the Brooklyn Navy Yard looking forward from about frame 106. The double bottom can be seen, which became fuel tanks. (NARA)

USS *IOWA*

The Navy proceeded to fine-tune its design and construction plans for battleship USS *Iowa*. To construct the ship, it selected the Brooklyn Navy Yard. The Navy owned the shipyard, which meant it could revise the ship's plans multiple times without incurring additional costs. Furthermore, the Navy could have the Brooklyn Navy Yard prepare the working construction plans for the three other forthcoming *Iowa*-class battleships: *New Jersey* (BB-62), *Missouri* (BB-63), and *Wisconsin* (BB-64).

The Brooklyn Navy Yard had significant experience in building battleships, having built eight battleships, starting with USS *Maine* in 1889. The other battleships were USS *Connecticut*, *Florida*, *New York*, *Arizona*, *New Mexico*, *Tennessee* (BB-43), and *North Carolina*. Based on the design of the machinery rooms of the *South Dakota* class, the four machinery rooms for BB-61 had been proposed at 64 feet in length. This represented

a major risk should a torpedo or a diving shell hit a bulkhead separating two machinery rooms. The result would be flooding of 128 feet of the ship's hull. The designers at the Brooklyn Navy Yard proposed, and the Navy agreed, to separate the fire room with two boilers from an engine room with one set of turbines, the main condensers, and supporting machinery. As a result, the original design of four large machinery rooms became eight spaces, each only 32 feet long, and the flooding risk was halved. Additionally, this structure reduced the number of breaks in the armored decks required for uptakes from the boilers to the funnels.

USS *Iowa* was laid down on 27 June 1940. The keel and the lower sections of the hull comprised a triple bottom with two layers of storage tanks that provided space for fuel oil, reserve feed, potable water, and aviation fluids. Storage of 9,520 tons of fuel oil gave the ship significant endurance for Pacific operations and

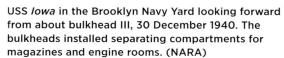

NAVY YARD N.Y. 12-30-40 U.S.S IOWA BB61
VIEW LOOKING FORWARD FROM ABOUT BULKHEAD III.
F111C 69

NAVY YARD N.Y. 9-30-40 U.S.S. IOWA BB61
VIEW LOOKING AFT FROM ABOUT FR. 101.
F111C20.

USS *Iowa* in the Brooklyn Navy Yard looking forward
from about bulkhead III, 30 December 1940. The
bulkheads installed separating compartments for
magazines and engine rooms. (NARA)

USS *Iowa* in the Brooklyn Navy Yard
looking forward from about frame 90.
The open turret barbette structures
have temporary covers. (NARA)

USS *Iowa* in the Brooklyn Navy Yard looking aft from about frame 101 (NARA)

USS *Iowa* in the Brooklyn Navy Yard midship looking forward. The armored barbettes for the two forward gun turrets are now in place. (NARA)

the ability to refuel destroyers. Nominal endurance at 12 knots was 18,000 nautical miles, and 15,900 nautical miles at 17 knots.

With the keel in place and the triple bottom constructed, the frames for the hull were attached and major lateral bulkheads were built. These bulkheads provided the internal separation for the structure of multiple spaces for boiler and engine rooms, magazines, and barbettes for the gun turrets. With the spaces delineated for the boiler and engine rooms, the boilers built by Babcock & Wilcox and the turbine sets built by GE could be lowered into place.

To provide the 33 knots required by the General Board, the *Iowa*'s propulsion plant was required to produce 212,000 shaft horsepower (shp), with an overload to 254,000 shp. The engine and boilers were designed to produce 245,000 shp if needed. The power was produced by eight boilers, with two boilers and all their supporting equipment positioned in each of the four firerooms. The boilers were a three-drum express type with a designed working pressure of 634 psi and an operating pressure of 565 psi. These boilers produced superheated steam of 850 degrees. The steam was delivered to the turbines by the main steam line to each of the four engine rooms. Each engine room contained a high-pressure turbine and a low-pressure turbine. A double reduction gear transferred the revolutions of the turbine to 202 rpm for the propellers. Each of the four engine rooms also contained a set of two turbo generators, which powered the electrical systems running the equipment that serviced all aspects of the ship's operations except the propulsion systems.

With the internal layout of the ship in process, the external skin plating could be attached to the internal framework. The design of the ship's armor protection was based on the principle of defending the ship against naval guns with the

(top) Hoisting one of the ship's nine 16-in/50-cal Mark 7 main battery guns on board while she was fitting out at the New York Navy Yard, circa autumn 1942. Another gun is still on the pier, at the bottom of the photo. (NARA)

(bottom) Installing the battleship's forward 16-in/50-cal gun turrets while she was fitting out at the Brooklyn Navy Yard, circa autumn 1942. View looks aft and to port, with the No. 2 turret in the center of the view and the forward fire-control tower at left. (NARA)

same caliber as those carried by the ship. To this end, an immune zone was calculated as lying between two ranges established for incoming direct (horizontal) fire and plunging (downward) fire, respectively. The inner range of the zone of immunity was set as the distance beyond which side armor could not be penetrated by direct enemy fire. This was calculated as 18,000 yards for a 16-inch/45-caliber 2,240-pound shell. The outer range was the shortest distance at which an enemy's falling shell could penetrate the target ship's deck armor. This was calculated as 30,000 yards for the above shell. After these calculations were made and the armor-protection design was finalized, a heavier shell weighing 2,700 pounds was introduced. The new shell shrank the calculated immune zone by pushing its inner range out to 20,200 yards and pulling its outer range closer to 25,500 yards. However, the armor plate for USS *Iowa* had already been ordered, and it was not possible to amend the design of the armor.

The armored belt was constructed to fit between the external skin plating and internal decks, with the armor plates angled inward at 19 degrees. The armored belt comprised an upper and a lower belt. The lower belt of class B armor was 12 inches thick at the top but thinned down to 1.6 inches where it met the triple bottom. The upper belt was class A armor, 12.1 inches thick and 10 feet 6 inches deep. The inclination of the armor belt at 19 degrees inward from the external hull plating had the effect of representing 13.5 inches of vertical armor but without the additional weight.

The total depth of the armor belt was 38 feet 6 inches and formed the citadel from frame 50, just forward of No. 1 barbette, to frame 166, just aft of No. 3 barbette. The length of the armored belt from frame 50 to frame 166 totaled 556 feet.

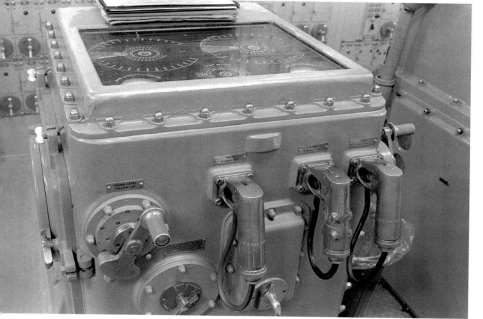

(top) A view of the closed breach on one of the Mark 7 16-in/50-cal guns on USS *Iowa*. (NARA)

(bottom) The Mark 6 stable element in the aft secondary battery plotting room of USS *Iowa*. Two of the three firing triggers are visible in the lower right of the photo. (NARA)

Two armored transverse bulkheads, at frames 50 and 166, respectively, completed the armored citadel of the ship. These bulkheads protected the ship from shells and bombs coming from ahead or aft. The armor on these transverse bulkheads was 11.3 inches thick, tapering to 8.5 inches at the bottom.

Armor protection was extended beyond the citadel aft, from frame 166 to frame 189 on the third deck, to cover the steering-gear leads and equipment. The steering-gear machinery and pistons between frames 189 and 203 were covered by 6.2 inches of class B armor.

Three horizontal armored decks completed the armor protection for USS *Iowa*. The main deck comprised the bomb deck of 1.5-inch class B armor. The bomb deck was intended to detonate general-purpose bombs on contact and to arm armor-piercing bombs prematurely, causing them to explode between the bomb deck and the main armor deck, thereby protecting the vital magazines and engine/boiler rooms.

The main armor deck was 4.75-inch class B armor laid on 1.25-inch special treatment steel (STS). This deck was designed to prevent plunging armor-piercing shells and bombs from reaching the ship's vital components. The splinter deck was 0.625 inches of STS, designed to capture splinters and spalling from explosions on the armor deck. The splinter deck is in effect a ceiling for the third deck, also composed of STS.

Torpedo bulkheads were installed between the inclined armor belt and the hull, starting at the third-deck level and joining the double bottom. The lower section of the armor belt comprised the third torpedo bulkhead. External to this bulkhead were two additional bulkheads that were attached to the double bottom. The voids between the hull and the torpedo bulkheads were filled with fuel oil, which was designed to absorb some of any explosive pressure.

The face plate of each turret was 17 inches of class B armor over 2.5 inches of STS. This combination was equal to a single plate 18.75 inches thick. The side plates of the turret were 9.5 inches of class A armor on 0.75 inches of STS. The rear plate of the turret was 12 inches of class A armor, whereas the turret roof was made from plates of class B armor 7.25 inches thick.

The three barbettes comprise multiple segments of class A armor and extend downward from the turret base plate to the main armored second deck. The segments facing the ship's beam were 17.3 inches thick. Facing forward and aft were segments 11.6 inches thick and 14.8 inches thick on the quarters. Between the main armor deck and the third deck, the armor of the barbette was 3 inches of STS plate.

The *Iowa* conning tower, for command-and-control during action, was three levels. The highest level comprised fire control with the director. The next level

The overall view of the aft secondary battery plotting room of USS *Iowa*. (NARA)

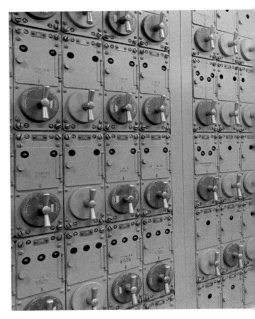

The switchboard in the aft secondary battery plotting room of USS *Iowa*. The switchboard controls which director controls which gun turret. (NARA)

down was for control of the ship with steering, engine room controls, and communications. The lower level was for admiral and flag staff.

Armor protection for the conning tower was class B armor 17.3 inches thick. The roof plates were 7.25-inch class B armor. The conning tower was connected to the armor citadel at the second-deck level by a vertical communications tube, the walls of which were 16-inch class B armor.

The main armament of USS *Iowa* comprised nine 16-inch/50-caliber guns, located in three gun turrets, two forward and one aft. Each gun had its own slide and elevating mechanism and therefore could be fired separately. Each gun was also served by its own projectile and powder hoist.

For each of the three gun turrets, 16-inch/50-caliber shells were stored vertically, base down, on two shell flats located below the gun mechanism. The shell flats each comprised three circular sections. The outer section was fixed to the cylindrical turret wall and stored projectiles in a double layer, against the wall, with each shell lashed in place by a chain around its base.

The central section of the shell flat did not hold any stored shells. It revolved with the gun turret, with the shell hoist tube fixed to it. This hoist elevated the shell vertically up a tube to the rear of the gun breech. The shell hoist tube became a cradle for the shell. The

cradle ended with the spanning tray in the gun turret, which pivoted with the shell from the vertical to the horizontal and became part of the loading tray for the shell to be rammed into the gun breech.

The inner section of the shell flat revolved with the gun turret. It was also independently powered so that it could be rotated in either direction to allow shells stored on this section to be lined up with the shell hoist for loading.

Projectiles from the outer and inner sections were moved on their bases to the central section by using the parbuckling capstan. The floor of all three sections was lightly oiled so the base of a shell could slide easily between the sections. A rope was passed around the rotating band of the shell, and the other end of the rope was attached to a revolving capstan whose movement made the shell slide onto the central section, where it was placed in the shell hoist and elevated to the gun house for loading.

Powder bags were stored in metal canisters in the turret's magazines, located on the third platform deck. When removed from the canister, the powder bags were placed by a powder man on a brass loading tray on a roller track and were moved by sliding them to a fireproof scuttle, where they passed from the magazine through the scuttle into an annular space.

The annular space between two circular armored bulkheads provided double fireproof separation of the

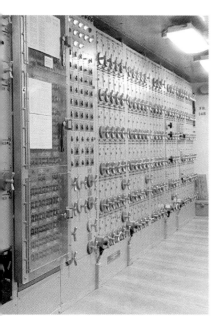

The Mark 8 fire-control computer in the aft main battery plotting room of USS *Iowa*. With the cover removed, the wheels and cogs of the mechanical workings are visible. (NARA)

magazine from the powder-handling room and turret mechanism. The powder magazine was on the outside of the bulkhead; the powder-handling room was on the inside of the second bulkhead. In the annular space, a powder man removed the powder bag from the magazine scuttle and passed it across the annular space and into another scuttle that reached into the powder-handling room. The powder bag was then hand-carried by a powder man in the powder-handling room to one of the three powder hoists that served the three turret guns. The central part of the floor of the powder-handling room with the powder-hoist mechanism was fixed to the turret's revolving structure so the powder hoist corresponded with the location of the rotating gun. Six powder bags were loaded onto two trays inside the powder car, which was then winched electronically up the dumbwaiter shaft to the gun house. The shaft opened to the side of the gun breech. The powder bags were then rolled out onto the loading tray, ready to be rammed into the gun breech.

The loading arrangement for the 16-inch/50-caliber gun was two rounds per minute. With nine rounds of shells weighing 2,700 pounds each, the USS *Iowa* could ideally place a total of 24,300 pounds of explosive shells on target every 30 seconds.

Local control in the gun turret provided backup fire control, but the main control for aiming and firing of the guns was located in the two plotting rooms, deep within the armor citadel on the third platform deck. These rooms contained a Mark 8 Ford rangekeeper, a Mark 41 stable vertical gyroscope with three pistol-grip firing keys, a Mark 48 bombardment computer, radar consoles, power supply, and the fire-control switchboard.

The plotting rooms received input for this equipment from the two Mark 38 directors, Spot 1 on top of the forward fire-control tower and Spot 2 on the aft fire-control tower. The directors used optical long-base, 26-foot-6-inch stereoscopic rangefinders to locate the target by line-of-sight, calculate the range and bearing of the target, and keep the target in sight with continuous updates. This information was transmitted to the plotting rooms and fed into the Ford rangekeeper, which then determined the elevation of the gun and the turret train to the angle of deflection needed for the shell, once fired, to meet the future position of the moving target. The rangekeeper could calculate firing solutions up to a target speed of 45 knots at a range of 50,000 yards.

The fire-control switchboard in the plotting room controlled the inputs and outputs of the fire-control system. As insurance in the event of any damage, the switchboard provided backup sources of information by routing data circuits to alternative systems.

The top level of the conning tower was Spot 3. It contained three periscopes for spotting targets. Spot 3 provided backup to the other spotting locations and provided additional input to the rangekeeper.

The three gun turrets carried either of two types of primary rangefinders: Turret 1 had a coincidence rangefinder, whereas turrets 2 and 3 had stereoscopic rangefinders. At 46 feet in length, each rangefinder was long-base, with 25 times magnification. The rangefinders were located in the rear of the turret running across the gun captain's area. Each rangefinder was stabilized to mitigate the movement of the ship, thus enabling the rangefinder operator to stay on target.

Each turret also carried four telescopes for sight pointers and sight setters. There were also two periscopes mounted in the turret roof for the use of the turret officer and turret captain. A Mark 3 rangekeeper was also located in the gun captain's area to provide the turret with full local control should input from the two plotting rooms not be available. The turret could also control the fire of the other turrets if necessary.

The Ford rangekeeper in the aft secondary battery plotting room of USS *Iowa*. (NARA)

Bird's-eye view of the amidships section of USS *Iowa*, circa February–March 1943. Four quad Bofor gun mounts are in place. (NavSource, U.S. Navy)

USS *Iowa* carried three Vought OS2U Kingfisher spotting aircraft on the fantail, which were launched from one of two catapults. The Kingfishers were used to locate the enemy at ranges beyond what could be seen from the fire-control towers. Once the enemy was located and taken under fire, the aircraft then spotted the fall of shot and reported by radio the aiming corrections required to bring shellfire onto the target.

In addition to the main armament, USS *Iowa* carried 20 5-inch/38-caliber dual-purpose guns for firing at surface, shore, and aircraft targets. These guns were carried in twin armored mounts, five per beam. Two mounts were located at the 01 level each side of the superstructure, and three mounts were located at the 02 level, again at each side of the superstructure.

USS *Iowa* being prepared for launch at the Brooklyn Navy Yard circa late August 1942. Note the heavy chains used to brake the ship after she had entered the water and men lounging at lower right, near a Navy Department safety poster, listening to a Marine Corps band. (NHHC)

Commissioning ceremony of USS *Iowa*, Brooklyn Navy Yard, New York, 22 February 1943. (NavSource, U.S. Navy)

USS *Iowa* in dry dock, Brooklyn Navy Yard. (Library of Congress)

The gun mount contained the two 5-inch guns and their respective slides, gun-laying mechanism, and fire-control equipment. The mount sat on a carriage, which comprised a heavy framework held by a base ring on which the mount revolved. A central column extended from the mount down to a handling room. Projectile and powder hoists were suspended from the mount's base ring, supported by the central column. The handling room carried the ready-service ammunition and in turn was supplied by dredger-type hoists from a magazine located on the third deck within the armored citadel.

The 5-inch/38-caliber guns were capable of a heavy rate of fire: an experienced gun crew could maintain a rate of fire between 15 and 22 rounds per minute. Control of this rate of gunfire was managed through three methods of fire control. The first was the primary control managed by the director, which signaled through the computer for train and elevation of the guns. The next method was a standby system in case of a loss of signal between the director and the computer. Information was then transferred from the director via telephone to the plotting room where gun orders originated and were transmitted to the guns. The third method was local control whereby the mount captain directed the pointer, trainer, and sight setter. The mount captain issued instructions for fuse setting and target selection.

The 5-inch/38-caliber gun was designed in 1932 and first installed on USS *Farragut* (DD-348) in 1934. The performance of the gun was exemplary and was eventually fitted to every major U.S. warship.

Of the four directors for the 5-inch/38-caliber guns, one was forward and one aft, with one on each beam. The directors were mounted as high as possible to enjoy the widest range of target angles with overlapping fields of view. Each director was fitted with a 15-foot base stereoscopic rangefinder with dual power of 12 or 24 magnification, and two telescopes. The director's control officer had a slewing sight to designate a target and communicate it to the other optics. A director also carried a Mark 4 radar with a roof-mounted antenna. The antenna was linked with the director's rangefinders and telescopes to support target tracking.

In addition to the fire-control equipment in the plotting room, the 5-inch/38-caliber system had a starshell computer. This computer sent starshell gun train, elevation, and fuze settings to the director, which had a starshell spot transmitter to send correction information for shell placement. Starshell placement was to set the starshell burst 1,000 yards beyond the target and 1,500 feet above the target.

The USS *Iowa's* secondary battery and fire-control system were of known effectiveness, as had been proven in the night battle of 15 November 1942, when USS *Washington* fought the Japanese battleship *Kirishima* and its accompanying cruisers, *Atago* and *Takao*. By effective use of radar, USS *Washington* used its main armament of 16-inch/45-caliber guns on *Kirishima*. It also used its aftmost 5-inch mounts to fire 62 starshells over *Kirishima* and its two forward starboard 5-inch mounts to launch a hail of 107 shells, with 40 5-inch shells hitting *Kirishima*. The *Washington* used its two remaining starboard 5-inch mounts to fire on *Atago* and *Takao* to divert their attention from *South Dakota*, which was able to withdraw from the battle. The ability to divide *Washington's* gunfire to multiple targets using multiple functions in a frenzied night battle was a battle-winning outcome.

Similarly, the experience gained weeks before at the Battle of Santa

USS *Iowa* looking aft from the forward fire-control tower during the ship's shakedown period, 1943. Carrier in the distance may be USS *Lexington* (CV-16). Photographed off Norfolk, Virginia, 18 May 1943. (NHHC)

Table 7: Comparison of *Iowa* BB-4 (1897) with *Iowa* BB-61 (1943)

Data Point	BB-4	BB-61
Laid down	5 August 1893	27 June 1940
Launched	28 March 1896	27 August 1942
Commissioned	16 June 1897	22 February 1943
Displacement	11,346 long tons	45,000 long tons
Length	362 ft 6-in	887 ft 3-in
Beam	72 ft 3-in	108 ft 2-in
Draft	28 ft	37-ft 2in
Power	11,000 shp	212,000 shp
Speed	17 knots	33 knots
Armament	4 × 12-in/35-cal 8 × 8-in/35-cal	9 × 16-in/50-cal 20 × 5-in/38-cal
Armor		
Belt	14-in	12-in
Barbettes	14-in	17.3-in
Turret	15-in	19.5-in
Conning Tower	10-in	17.3-in
Deck	3-in	4.75-in

Cruz was used in configuring the antiaircraft armament for USS *Iowa*. That battle on 26 October 1942 pitted *South Dakota* and *Enterprise* against multiple dive- and torpedo-bomber attacks launched by the Japanese aircraft carriers *Zuikaku* and *Junyo*. While *South Dakota* and *Enterprise* both suffered damage from these attacks, their collective antiaircraft fire from 40-mm Bofor and 20-mm Oerlikon guns claimed a large number of Japanese attacking aircraft. The *South Dakota* alone claimed 26 downed aircraft. Both *Enterprise* and *South Dakota* had been recently equipped with these guns while at Pearl Harbor for repairs. Accordingly, the *Iowa* was fitted with 15 quad Bofor guns and 60 single Oerlikon guns at the time of her commissioning.

USS *Iowa* was commissioned on 22 February 1943, seven months ahead of schedule. The Brooklyn Navy Yard had employed subassembly shops to build sections of the ship, which were then hoisted into place by overhead cranes. This subassembly process, together with welding rather than riveting, reduced construction times. The yard's subassembly shops, structural shops, mold lofts, and machine shops all played significant roles in building ships faster.

On 24 February 1943, Captain John McCrea conned USS *Iowa* out of New York harbor, into the Atlantic, heading toward Chesapeake Bay for the shakedown cruise. The *Iowa* now bristled with radar antennas. Radar antennas for fire control were located on top of

the conning tower and the Spot 3 director. The main directors, Spots 1 and 2, were fitted with Mark 3 radar antennas following the shakedown cruise. Included also were an SK air-search antenna, carried on a single-pole foretopmast attached to the rear of the fire-control tower, and the SG surface-search antenna, mounted on a bracket extending forward from the fire-control tower just below the air-defense platform. During the war, USS *Iowa*'s radar suite would be upgraded as new equipment was developed.

Effective as of 27 August 1943, the shakedown cruise had tested all of *Iowa*'s armaments as well as the interface between the many systems that managed and directed the armaments and powered the ship. The *Iowa* sailed into the North Atlantic to join the naval force guarding against the German battleship *Tirpitz* as Allied convoys sailed to Russia with war supplies. This potentially pitted the USS *Iowa* against *Tirpitz*, a battleship of roughly comparable size but slower than *Iowa* and with eight 15-inch guns versus nine 16-inch guns.

Fortunately for *Tirpitz*, a duel with *Iowa* and her 16-inch guns with heavy shells was avoided. Two Royal Navy midget submarines, X-6 and X-7, exploded four mines near and underneath the hull of *Tirpitz* in September 1943, causing sufficient damage to prevent her from sailing for more than six months. The *Iowa* returned to the Norfolk Navy Yard for maintenance and repairs on 23 October 1943.

CONVEYING PRESIDENT ROOSEVELT

During the night of 13 November 1943, the USS *Iowa* set sail with very important passengers from Hampton Roads, bound for Mers-el-Kébir, in Algeria. The *Iowa* was conveying President Franklin Roosevelt to North Africa as his first stop on the way to Cairo and Tehran to join British Prime Minister Winston Churchill, Chinese leader Chiang Kai-Shek, and Soviet leader Joseph Stalin for their war-planning conference. In addition to the president, *Iowa* also carried Secretary of State Cordell Hull, presidential adviser Harry Hopkins, the Joint Chiefs of Staff—Admiral William D. Leahy, Admiral Ernest J. King, General George C. Marshall, and General Henry H. "Hap" Arnold—and their staff members.

President Roosevelt's polio made it difficult for him to move about or even stand. So at the Norfolk Navy Yard, temporary elevators were installed to enable the president to move between decks, and a bathtub was added to the president's quarters—the only bathtub installed in a U.S. Navy ship. The presidential bathtub later served another purpose when it was used as a prize for a lottery in 1952 to raise money from the ship's crew for the Navy Relief Society. The winner of the lottery could take a bath in the captain's cabin bathtub.

Escorted by three destroyers, and with air coverage provided by two escort carriers, USS *Block Island* (CVE-21) and *Santee* (CVE-29), the *Iowa* sailed across the Atlantic, untroubled by U-boats and their torpedoes. However, a torpedo attack on the *Iowa* did occur because of a missed firing primer for a torpedo tube on board the destroyer USS *William D. Porter* (DD-579).

On 14 November the president had asked to see the *Iowa*'s antiaircraft guns in action. With the presidential party on deck, target balloons were released, soon followed by vigorous gunfire. The *William D. Porter* also took the opportunity to conduct a torpedo drill, but when a seaman forgot to remove a firing primer from one of the ship's torpedo tubes, a live torpedo was launched at the *Iowa* along with its crew and distinguished passengers. After some urgent signals between the ships, *Iowa* turned sharply toward the destroyer and increased to full power, with the aft antiaircraft guns now firing at the approaching torpedo rather than at the balloons. The turn by *Iowa* was so

USS *Iowa* delivering President Franklin Roosevelt to Africa for transit to the Tehran Conference, Mers-el-Kébir, Oran, Algeria, 20 November 1943. Note French cruiser *Jeanne d'Arc* just beyond *Iowa*. (USS *Iowa*)

Table 8: USS *Iowa* Miles Sailed and Average Speed, 4 October–6 December 1943

From / To	Distance (miles)	Average Speed (knots)
Hampton Roads, Virginia / Mers-el-Kébir, Algeria	4,217.6	24.64
Mers-el-Kébir, Algeria / Bahia, Brazil	4,467.5	20.91
Bahia, Brazil / Freetown, Sierra Leone	2,217.6	22.60
Freetown, Sierra Leone / Dakar, Senegal	1,316.6	19.56
Dakar, Senegal / Potomac River Anchorage	3,941.8	23.56

SOURCE: REPORT BY CAPT JOHN L. MCCREA

sharp that the president's Secret Service staff had to grip his wheelchair tightly to prevent it from running overboard. The torpedo exploded in the turbulent wake of the *Iowa*. After the excitement had passed, President Roosevelt stated that no one was to be punished for the incident. However, after returning to Bermuda, the *William D. Porter* was ordered to the Aleutians, well away from both President Roosevelt and USS *Iowa*.

USS *Iowa* passed through the Strait of Gibraltar and sailed into the Mediterranean at night. However, Spanish searchlights highlighted the ships, compromising the secrecy of the ships' movements. The timetable for the president's visit was shortened as a result. The president left *Iowa* at Mers-el-Kébir at 0842 on 20 November.

USS *Iowa* passed safely back through the Strait of Gibraltar into the Atlantic on the evening of 20 November, accompanied by HMS *Sheffield* and destroyers from both the U.S. Navy and Royal Navy. She crossed the equator and anchored off Bahia, Brazil, on 30 November. The ship took on 1,323,050 gallons of fuel

oil from the SS *Malaya* before recrossing the Atlantic to Dakar, Senegal. The anchorage at Dakar was difficult for the *Iowa* as the protection from German submarines was minimal. Therefore, *Iowa* sailed on to Freetown, Sierra Leone, a major Royal Navy base on the African west coast, where she could anchor in the river behind submarine nets. The ship left Freetown on 6 December, sailed back to Dakar, and on 9 December was on station to meet President Roosevelt, who was arriving by air that day from Tehran. The president and his party boarded the ship at 2000 hours, and the *Iowa* sailed at 2100 hours for the return journey to Washington, D.C. On 16 December 1943 President Roosevelt disembarked from the *Iowa* and boarded his yacht, *Potomac*, off Cherry Point, Virginia, for the balance of his journey up the Potomac River to the White House.

The double round-trip crossing of the Atlantic at 25 knots proved the reliability of the *Iowa*'s machinery. The 16,161 miles that *Iowa* sailed also allowed the officers and crew to exercise their gun skills and practice their underway watches.

WORLD WAR II IN THE PACIFIC

On 2 January 1944, USS *Iowa* sailed from Hampton Roads and joined up with her sister ship USS *New Jersey*, the second ship of the *Iowa* class, which had just completed her shakedown cruise. Together, under the command of Rear Admiral Olaf Hustvedt, the ships formed Battleship Division 7, with *Iowa* as flagship. On passing through the Panama Canal and entering the Pacific, the two ships joined the U.S. Fifth Fleet under the command of Admiral Raymond A. Spruance. This Fleet was under the command of Admiral Chester Nimitz, Commander-in-Chief of the U.S. Pacific Fleet.

Formed on 5 August 1943, the Fifth Fleet had steadily grown as fast battleships and *Essex*-class fast aircraft carriers were built in U.S. shipyards and joined the fleets after their shakedown cruises. This Fleet was the core of Admiral Nimitz's planned Central Pacific Drive to defeat Japan.

The *Iowa* and *New Jersey* arrived at the atoll of Funafuti. They joined the Fleet in preparing for the advance on the Marshall Islands and took up their roles in support of the fast carriers. These carriers attacked the atolls of Kwajalein and Eniwetok in the Marshall Islands, destroying Japanese aircraft and defense positions ahead of the Marines who landed from the sea and occupied the islands.

OPERATION HAILSTONE

Admiral Spruance was concerned that the Japanese-controlled island of Truk in the Caroline Island chain could threaten the Fifth Fleet advance against Eniwetok. Truk Lagoon had been used as a major naval base for the Japanese Combined Fleet, including the battleships *Yamato* and *Musashi*, in support of Japanese activities throughout the South Pacific. Truk was therefore sometimes called the "Gibraltar of the Pacific." Thinking it might be possible to catch major units of the Japanese navy in Truk Lagoon, Admiral Spruance launched Operation Hailstone.

The operation comprised six fast battleships: USS *Iowa*, *New Jersey*, *Massachusetts*, *Alabama*, *South Dakota*, and *North Carolina*. Five fleet carriers—USS *Enterprise*, *Yorktown* (CV-5), *Essex* (CV-9), *Intrepid* (CV-11), and *Bunker Hill* (CV-17)—provided more than 500 aircraft. The objective of Operation Hailstone was to sink as many ships as possible at the lagoon and destroy onshore naval-support buildings and facilities, but not to invade and occupy the atoll. Truk was to be damaged, isolated, and left to "wither on the vine" behind the advancing U.S. Navy.

Admiral Spruance took command of the operation on board the *New Jersey*. He was advised by aircraft that several Japanese warships were fleeing Truk through the lagoon's northern exit. Spruance formed Task Group 50.9 and on 17 February 1944 set off in pursuit with the battleships *New Jersey* and *Iowa*, cruisers *Minneapolis* (CA-36) and *New Orleans* (CA-32), and destroyers *Charrette* (DD-581), *Burns* (DD-588), *Izard* (DD-589), and *Bradford* (DD-545). Aircraft from the carrier *Bunker Hill* provided air cover.

At 1318 local time, a Japanese aircraft appeared through a hole in a thick overhang of clouds and dropped a bomb at the *Iowa*. The bomb exploded on line with the No. 1 turret just off the starboard beam, sending a soaking spray onto deck gunners and bridge crew. The aircraft then attempted a strafing attack but flew off when dissuaded by fire from the ship's 5-inch and 20-mm guns.

At 1414 Spot 1 sighted an unidentified burning ship, range 25 miles. At 1500 three additional targets were sighted: a cruiser at 33,000 yards as well as a destroyer of the *Fubuki* class and another small ship at 22,000 yards. Spot 1 identified the cruiser as of the *Aoba* class. At 1510 the American destroyers opened fire on the small ship, identified as a *Nasami*-class minelayer.

At 1516 Admiral Spruance ordered the cruisers *Minneapolis* and *New Orleans* to close and destroy the *Aoba*-class cruiser, later identified as *Katori*, and then rejoin the task group. *Iowa* opened fire on *Katori* with 5-inch mounts and 16-inch guns at 1530. The 5-inch mounts fired 124 shells. The 16-inch guns fired 46 projectiles in eight salvos, which all straddled the

Ships of the U.S. Pacific Fleet anchored at Majuro 25 April 1944, shortly before leaving to attack Truk. USS *Enterprise* (CV-6) is at right, with four *Essex*-class carriers beyond her. Battleships at left include USS *Iowa* and *New Jersey* (BB-62). There are three other fast battleships and three light carriers present, as well as several old battleships, cruisers, and auxiliaries. (NHHC)

USS *Iowa* anchored at Majuro Atoll, April 1944.
Photo taken from the USS *Essex* (CV-9). (NHHC)

target. Just after the fourth straddle fell, the target took on a heavy list to port. At 1541 her bow rose 30 feet out of the water and *Katori* sank stern first.

During this engagement three torpedo tracks were seen heading for *Iowa*. One torpedo passed close down the port side from ahead. A second torpedo passed close under the stern. A third passed about 200 yards ahead on the port bow, broached, and continued on the surface to starboard. In accordance with standing orders not to wait for an order to open fire when a torpedo was sighted, the starboard 5-inch, 40-mm, and 20-mm batteries opened fire on the passing torpedo.

At 1539 the Japanese destroyer, under continuous fire from *New Jersey* off the port beam of *Iowa*, rolled over and sank rapidly, leaving a large area of burning oil. The Japanese destroyer *Nowaki* headed westward, chased by the two U.S. battleships, with *Iowa* attaining a speed of 32.5 knots. *Nowaki* was ranged at 35,700 yards, and at 1547 *Iowa* fired five main-battery salvos at her. As the target changed course and disappeared into the glare of the setting sun, *Iowa*'s radar was able to range on *Nowaki*'s mast top and fire a last salvo at 39,000 yards. However, the *Nowaki* escaped. Both battleships ceased fire at 1558.

Given the military and political significance of Truk, Admiral Spruance wanted to drive home the significance of Operation Hailstone to both his sailors and the enemy. He directed *Iowa* and *New Jersey* to hoist the largest Stars and Stripes they carried. So adorned, Task Group 50.9 sailed completely around Truk, the Japanese Gibraltar of the Pacific, and met back with Task Force 58 at 0500 northeast of Truk.

Operation Hailstone was the first naval operation in which USS *Iowa* engaged the enemy with all her armaments and used her electronic, radar, and communications equipment to manage and operate all her systems. The ship's engines and boilers operated at high speed throughout the operation.

This test of *Iowa*'s crew and systems threw up a series of small issues that needed addressing. For the main

Crew for the 20-mm Oerlikon cannon engage in an antiaircraft exercise on USS *Iowa*, May 1943. (NavSource, U.S. Navy)

The forward port side Mark 28 5-in/38-cal gun mount on USS *Iowa*. (NARA)

USS *Iowa* fires a salvo from her aft 16-in turret during the bombardment of Tinian, 14–15 June 1944. (NHHC)

armament, the center gun of turret 2 failed to fire on the first salvo because of a failure of the firing lock, which was replaced. After main armament firing had ceased, a small burr was noted on the breech plug of the left gun of turret 3. This was probably caused by too high air pressure on the plug-closing system. The burr was honed down.

The crew were at general quarters for 27 hours. Turret crews were released on deck during lulls in action, and four meals were served by battle-mess men. Ventilation in closed compartments became an issue. The Combat Information Center (CIC) space was identified as inadequate for the necessary number of officers and crew occupying it. Senior officers were unable to move freely between plotting boards to maintain their awareness of tactical developments. For most CIC men, there was only standing room, which became tiring after prolonged general quarters. Workspace for taking notes and working codes was too small, so CIC staff used the adjacent captain's sea cabin for desk space.

The SG radar stopped working for ten minutes when vacuum tubes were shocked out of their sockets because of gunfire. The FH antenna continued to work notwithstanding that 39 bolts holding the polyrods were sheared off because of gunfire pressure.

Two main-drain pumps had failed during cruising. As a result, Iowa went into action with only three working main-drain pumps. The defective pumps were rebuilt by onboard engineering staff as a temporary solution.

The Iowa served as fighter director for a short period when New Jersey was unable to fulfill her designated role because of problems with her VHF transmitter. In this role, when her SK radar identified an enemy aircraft at 32 miles, the Iowa vectored fighters from the carrier USS Cowpens (CVL-25), which shot down the floatplane.

The action around Truk and the firing of the main 16-inch guns at the cruiser Katori and the destroyer Nowaki marked the only time the main guns of the Iowa were fired at enemy warships.

MILI ATOLL AND PONAPE

With Operation Hailstone successfully completed, the two resupplied battleships Iowa and New Jersey sailed for the Marshall atoll of Mili where they were to practice shore bombardment. Naval gunnery was predicated upon one ship firing at another. The Ford Mark 8 rangekeeper fitted to both ships was the primary analog mechanical computer developed to integrate all the different calculations of range, heading, and speed of target, along with the firing ship's own speed, gun ware, temperature, and air pressure, and thereby calculate the required bearing and elevation of the guns so the fired projectiles would meet the target at a projected future position.

Shore bombardment was significantly less complex as the target was stationary, at a fixed elevation, and at a range that could be determined readily and accurately. The only variable was the ship's movements during firing. This meant that the main plot, the ship's navigator, and the crew of the Kingfisher spotting aircraft needed an accurate navigational chart showing the ship's planned track and the target area on land. In addition, a map of the target area was overlaid with a numbered grid to provide coordinates for fixing a target's position. The bombarding ship had to be navigated precisely, and its position had to be determined every few minutes. The range and bearing to the target were calculated on the navigation chart and that data provided the input to the Ford Mark 8 rangekeeper rather than the directors and radar plot. This system did not allow for rapid and continuous gunfire. The Kingfisher spotting aircraft had to call the location of the fall of shot by reference to the target area map and grid reference. Suggested corrections for placing the shot pattern on target were radioed back to the ship for input to the navigation chart and then into the rangekeeper, hence the need for practice at shore bombardment.

On 18 March 1944 with gunnery practice complete, bombardment of Mili Atoll at a range of 15,000 yards commenced with Iowa and New Jersey each fired four three-gun salvos during alternate ten-minute periods. The ships' Kingfisher aircraft spotted for range and Spot 1 provided the deflection detail. The two battleships destroyed a large building and ammunition dump. They then moved to bombard a coast-defense battery of four

16-in projectiles are staged on the forecastle for offloading from USS *Iowa*. (NARA)

4.7-inch guns, which returned fire. The *Iowa* was hit twice. The first hit was against the left side of turret 2. Fragments from the exploding shell demolished the sight port of the pointer's telescope. The left window of the Mark 52 rangefinder was likewise lost to enemy fire. Additionally, the weather and gas seal on the turret's left side was torn off for a distance of 20 feet and the splinter shield of the starboard-side 40-mm mount was peppered with fragments.

The second shell exploded on impact with the hull four feet below the main deck at frame 134, creating a hole 30 inches by 50 inches in the ship's side and damaging an air-escape line from a fuel-oil overflow line. The shell did not penetrate the inboard armored-torpedo bulkhead. In addition to the two hits, the Japanese gunners landed 20 shells within 500 yards of *Iowa*. The ship withdrew to a range of 20,000 yards, beyond the range of the 4.7-inch gun. The gunnery officer of *Iowa* stated that using high-capacity shells was a mistake, as the 180 projectiles fired did not penetrate and destroy the concrete gun emplacement but only caused a lot of smoke and dust.

The next bombardment took place on 1 May 1944 against the island of Ponape in the Carolines, where the Japanese had built an airfield with three runways. USS *Iowa* comprehensively damaged the runways from one end to the other by gunfire. Barracks, stores, and an army headquarters building for the island were also destroyed by gunfire. The island was defended by old (1902) Armstrong Whitworth naval 6-inch guns. However, to preserve defensive capacity against an invasion, which the battleships did not represent at that moment, the guns did not return fire at the battleships. Ponape was not invaded by the Marines but was isolated from resupply as the Central Pacific Drive moved westward and the United States commanded both air and sea access to Ponape.

UNITED STATES NAVAL INSTITUTE

View of the side of 16-in gun turret 2 showing point of impact of a Japanese 4.7-in projectile on the turret armor and the resulting damage to the light metal water seal. Damage occurred during the bombardment of Mili Atoll, 18 March 1944. (NHHC)

BATTLE OF THE PHILIPPINE SEA

Between the attacks on Mili and Ponape, the U.S. Fifth Fleet undertook a series of operations against Japanese-held islands and the New Guinea coast to support General Douglas MacArthur's advance toward the Philippines. These operations created two opportunities for the Japanese Combined Fleet and the Fifth Fleet to engage each other, but only one resulted in fleet surface actions.

The attacks on Guam, Saipan, and Tinian brought the Japanese Mobile Fleet, under the command of Admiral Jisaburō Ozawa, away from its base in the Tiwi Islands and the Philippines and into the Philippine Sea. The Japanese saw the advance by the U.S. Navy as an opportunity for the "single decisive engagement" that was the bedrock of Japanese naval strategy. A victory in such a massive engagement would represent Japan's optimum path to winning the war.

With the Philippines behind him, Admiral Ozawa's battle strategy was to pinch the Fifth Fleet between the Japanese air bases on Guam and the Japanese fleet, consisting of nine aircraft carriers—*Taiho, Chitose, Chiyoda, Zuiho, Shokaku, Zuikaku, Ryuho, Yunyo,* and *Hiyo*—and their complement of 450 aircraft. This formidable group of aircraft carriers was supported by the five battleships, *Yamato, Musashi, Kongo, Haruna,* and *Nagato.*

Fire-control technicians man SKY-4, the aft 5-in gun director on USS *Iowa*. (NARA)

Admiral Ozawa would have a tactical advantage by doubling the attacking runs of his carrier aircraft. After the aircraft were launched eastward from the carriers, they would attack the Fifth Fleet carriers and land beyond them, on Guam. There they would briefly refuel and rearm and then reattack the U.S. carriers as they flew westward back to their carriers. The 300 land-based bombers and fighters on Guam would also join the attack on the U.S. carriers. However, Ozawa's seemingly sound strategy foundered on the combined strengths of the Fifth Fleet's CIC radar vectoring, its battle-trained pilots flying Hellcat fighters, and the antiaircraft fire of fast battleships armed with proximity-fuzed shells.

Admiral Spruance had 15 aircraft carriers with 902 aircraft available to him, and 7 fast battleships, including *Iowa*. The aircraft carriers were organized into four task groups. Task Force 58.1 comprised USS *Hornet*, *Yorktown*, *Belleau Woods* (CVL-24), and *Bataan* (CVL-29). Carriers USS *Bunker Hill*, *Wasp* (CV-18), *Cabot*, and *Monterey* (CVL-26) were in Task Force 58.2, whereas Task Force 58.3 contained USS *Enterprise*, *Lexington*, *San Jacinto* (CVL-30), and *Princeton* (CV-37). Task Force 58.4 included USS *Essex*, *Langley*, and *Cowpens*. Each task group sailed in a circular formation.

The fast battleships were separated from their usual role of providing antiaircraft support for the aircraft carriers and were instead concentrated into their own group, Task Group 7, under the command of Admiral Willis A. Lee Jr. and comprising USS *Iowa*, *New Jersey*, *Washington*, *North Carolina*, *South Dakota*, and *Alabama*, with *Indiana* as the task-group guide in the center of the circular formation. The group was positioned 15 miles ahead of the four aircraft carriers of Task Force 58.3 so it could provide an antiaircraft screen for the carriers and rapidly undertake surface actions with the enemy fleet.

The position of the Japanese Mobile Fleet was known by the early morning of 18 June 1944, thanks to reports by U.S. submarines and intercepts of Japanese radio transmissions. Admiral Marc Mitscher, commander of the carrier task groups, planned a rapid advance during the morning so that the combined aircraft carriers of the task group could launch a major attack in the afternoon on the nine Japanese carriers. Following the carrier aircraft attacks, Admiral Mitscher considered a plan by which fast battleships would continue with after-dark attacks, relying on their search and fire-control radars to complete the destruction of the Mobile Fleet, and particularly any still-floating Japanese carriers.

Admiral Mitscher signaled Admiral Lee, "Do you desire night engagement?" Admiral Lee signaled back, "Do not (repeat not) believe we should seek night engagement. Possible advantages of radar more than offset by difficulties of communication and lack of training in fleet tactics at night. Would press pursuit of damaged or fleeing enemy, however, at any time." As a result of this exchange and Admiral Spruance's battle plan, Admiral Mitscher ordered his task groups to retire eastward toward Saipan to cover the Saipan invasion force and their transports. Admiral Mitscher was aware that, because of this move, his carriers were vulnerable to air attack from the Japanese carriers, and that the range from his carriers to the enemy carriers was too far for his carrier bombers to respond.

At 0600 on 19 June 1944, an Aichi D3A2 "Val" dive-bomber flying from Guam descended on Task Group 7 and was promptly shot down by the task group's screen of destroyers. At 1000 large numbers of enemy aircraft were spotted by radar 130 miles to the west. This prompted the launch of carrier Hellcat fighters that intercepted the enemy fighters, dive-bombers, and torpedo-bombers about 35 miles west of Task Group 7. Large numbers of enemy aircraft were shot down by carrier fighters. During the day approximately a dozen Japanese aircraft attacked the fast battleships, with nine of them shot down by the ships' antiaircraft guns. Only *South Dakota* was damaged in these attacks, when at 1049 a 500-pound bomb struck the port side of her superstructure, killing 24 and wounding 27. A torpedo plane crashed into and bounced off the starboard quarter at the waterline of *Indiana*, leaving a dent in the ship's outer hull plating.

The Battle of the Philippine Sea was primarily an air battle between Fifth Fleet aircraft carriers and those of the Japanese Mobile Fleet, with significant impact by two U.S. submarines, USS *Albacore* (SS-218) and *Cavalla* (SS-244).

For the USS *Iowa*, the battle involved four actions with Japanese aircraft. At 1050 a Kawaski Ki-48 twin bomber, referred to as a "Lilly," was spotted at 5,000 yards flying low and fast, judged at 205 mph. The Lilly was tracked by four 5-inch/38-caliber mounts for 15 seconds. The guns then opened with rapid continuous fire for 20 seconds, expending 20 5-inch shells, which caused the aircraft to catch fire and crash into the sea.

At 1100 two aircraft were spotted at 10,000 yards and were identified as a Zero fighter and a Val dive-bomber. Two mounts of four 5-inch/38-caliber guns under control by a director in semiautomatic mode

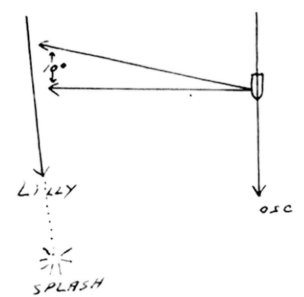

This diagram, prepared by an air-defense officer, shows the relative positions of the *Iowa* and an attacking *Kawaski Ki-48* ("Lilly") twin bomber shot down by the ship during the Battle of the Philippine Sea, 19 June 1944. (War Diary of USS *Iowa*)

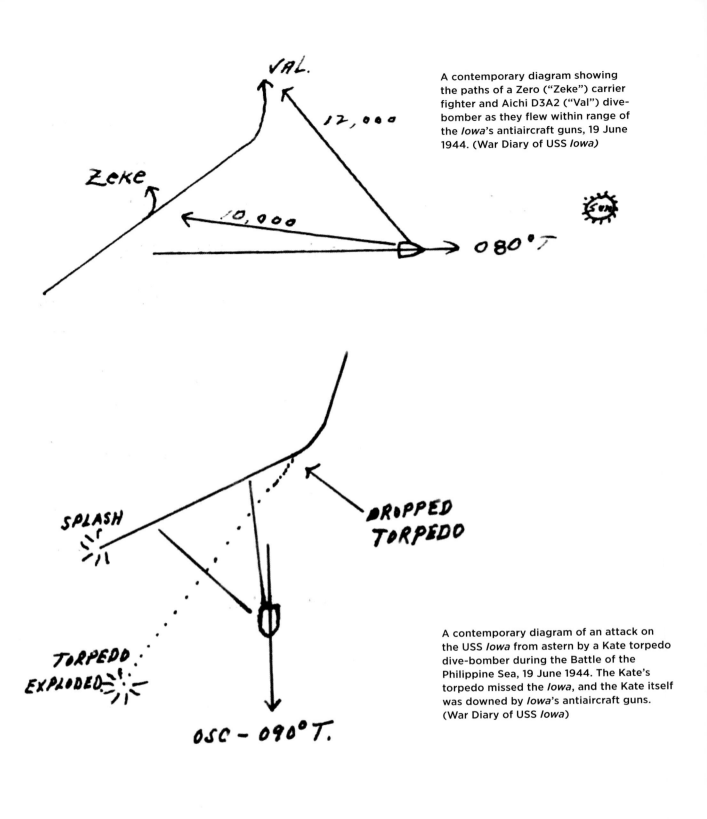

VAL.

12,000

Zeke

10,000

080°T

A contemporary diagram showing
the paths of a Zero ("Zeke") carrier
fighter and Aichi D3A2 ("Val") dive-
bomber as they flew within range of
the *Iowa*'s antiaircraft guns, 19 June
1944. (War Diary of USS *Iowa*)

SPLASH

DROPPED
TORPEDO

TORPEDO
EXPLODED

OSC – 090°T.

A contemporary diagram of an attack on
the USS *Iowa* from astern by a Kate torpedo
dive-bomber during the Battle of the
Philippine Sea, 19 June 1944. The Kate's
torpedo missed the *Iowa*, and the Kate itself
was downed by *Iowa*'s antiaircraft guns.
(War Diary of USS *Iowa*)

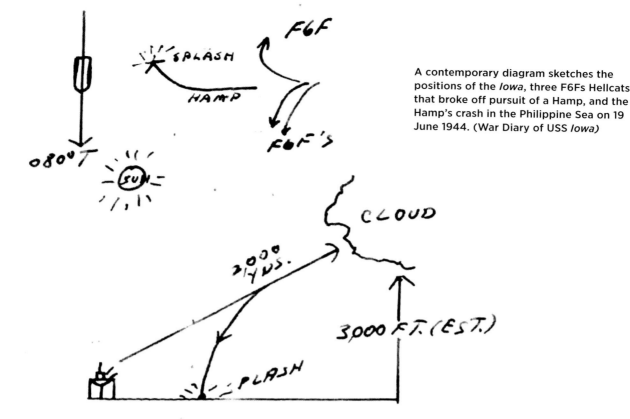

A contemporary diagram sketches the positions of the *Iowa*, three F6Fs Hellcats that broke off pursuit of a Hamp, and the Hamp's crash in the Philippine Sea on 19 June 1944. (War Diary of USS *Iowa*)

maintained rapid and continuous fire of 100 5-inch shells. The Zero turned away as soon as fire was opened. The Val continued on its flight pass up the port side of the *Iowa* at a distance of 10,000 yards, then turned to its left and changed altitude, disappearing from view. During firing, the hot-case chute that expelled propellant cases after being fired jammed in mount No. 8 and had to be cleared before firing could be resumed.

At 1200 a Nakajima B5N "Kate" carrier-based torpedo bomber was spotted flying very low and fast at 5,000 yards. Within five seconds of spotting the planes, the 5-inch/38-caliber mounts opened fire with 34 5-inch shells. Hits were observed within a further 10 seconds. The Kate cut under the USS *Iowa*'s stern and launched its torpedo as 40-mm guns fired 475 shells. Their tracer shells hit the Kate's fuselage near the cockpit. Two hundred 20-mm shells were also fired. The Kate dropped off on its right wing and splashed without burning. The torpedo run, estimated at about 1,800 yards, missed the ship by a wide margin. The torpedo exploded at the end of the run.

At 1325 a Mitsubishi A6M3 clipped-wing Zero ("Hamp") was sighted at 2,000 yards, emerging from a cloud base at 3,000 feet. It was diving directly at USS *Iowa* at about 300 mph. Three Grumman F6F Hellcats were chasing it and firing on its tail. The Hellcats broke away and the ship's 40-mm quads took over with rapid fire of 170 shells within three seconds. The 20-mm guns

fired 500 shells. The Hamp went into a slow roll. It smoked but did not burn and splashed 1,000 yards abaft the ship's port beam.

The USS *Iowa*'s contacts with the enemy on 19 June provide a brief insight into the speed—just a few seconds—within which attacking aircraft were spotted and brought under coordinated massive firepower. The rapid responses are a testament to the fire-control directors, system, equipment, and training of the gunners on board the *Iowa*.

While the ships of Task Group 7 maneuvered and defended themselves against Japanese bombers and torpedo planes, overhead the pilots of Japanese and American carrier aircraft fought their deadly duels with each other. Superior pilot skills, better aircraft, and efficient fighter direction married to radar made the air battle one sided. More than 350 Japanese aircraft were destroyed, with lack of armor and self-sealing fuel tanks contributing to their vulnerability. The battle would be nicknamed the "Marianas Turkey Shoot" after a returning pilot likened the ease of shooting down several Japanese planes to hunting turkeys back home.

That evening Admiral Spruance was certain that the Japanese fleet could not interfere with the landings on Saipan and the armada of transports delivering ammunition and supplies to the invasion ground troops. Accordingly, he gave permission to Admiral Mitscher to take most of his task groups northwest and locate

USS *Iowa* under way at sea during the Marshalls Operation, 24 January 1944. She is wearing Camouflage Measure 32, Design 1B. In the left distance, also painted in Camouflage Measure 32 (possibly Design 11D), is USS *Indiana* (BB-58). (NARA)

the Japanese Mobile Fleet. In addition to losing 350 aircraft, Admiral Ozawa had lost two aircraft carriers to U.S. submarines. USS *Albacore* had torpedoed *Taiho*, Ozawa's flagship, and USS *Cavalla* had torpedoed *Shokaku*. Both carriers sank.

In the afternoon of 29 June, aircraft from USS *Enterprise* located Admiral Ozawa's ships 275 miles from Admiral Mitscher's task groups. Despite the round-trip distance to the Japanese ships, ensuring that returning aircraft would have to land on his carriers at night, Admiral Mitscher ordered his carriers to attack. The air attack sank the carrier *Hiyo* and damaged three other carriers, but the Mobile Fleet escaped into the dark. Admiral Lee and Task Group 7 with USS *Iowa* gave chase all night but did not catch Admiral Ozawa and the three remaining carriers. The attack on the Mobile Fleet cost Admiral Mitscher the loss of 20 aircraft in combat and an additional 80

aircraft lost, chiefly from ditching in the sea as aircraft ran out of fuel.

The strategy for both the U.S. Navy and Japanese Navy following the Pearl Harbor attack was that aircraft carriers, if present, were the major objective of any naval action. The sinking of aircraft carriers dominated planning and then tactical operations. The escape of three Japanese aircraft carriers was a significant factor for future plans.

Following the chase of the Japanese fleet, the Fifth Fleet regrouped, refueled, and took on ammunition and supplies. The *Iowa* returned to her role of providing antiaircraft support to the aircraft carriers along with shore bombardments in the Marianas, the Carolines, and the Ryukyus. *Iowa* bombarded Saipan and Tinian of the Marianas on 13 June 1944. The capture of Saipan in early July provided a close anchorage for resupplying U.S. warships during the ongoing actions to suppress Japanese reinforcements to these islands.

THE BATTLE OF LEYTE GULF

In August 1944 Admiral William "Bull" Halsey Jr. replaced Admiral Spruance and the Fifth Fleet became the Third Fleet. The new name reflected the change in commanders but not the ships that constituted the fleet. This change coincided with a thrust to invade the Philippines, in which the Third Fleet was charged with neutralizing Japanese airfields in surrounding locations to minimize the Japanese ability to ferry aircraft to the Philippines.

On 6 October 1944 the *Iowa* sailed from the Ulithi Atoll anchorage as a unit of Task Group 38.2 under the command of Admiral Gerald F. Bogan, on board USS *Intrepid*. Task Group 38.2 also comprised the aircraft carriers USS *Bunker Hill*, *Hancock* (CV-19), *Cabot* (CVL-28), and *Independence* (CVL-22); the

fast battleship USS *New Jersey*; the cruisers USS *Vincennes* (CL-64), *Houston* (CL-81), and *Miami* (CL-89); and the two antiaircraft cruisers USS *San Diego* (CL-53) and *Oakland* (CL-95). Eighteen destroyers formed the screen for the task group. Admiral Bogan's task group joined Task Groups 38.1, 38.3, and 38.4 to form Task Force 38, which thus comprised 16 aircraft carriers, 6 fast battleships, 15 cruisers, and 48 destroyers. Admiral Marc Mitscher was in tactical command of Task Force 38, and Admiral Halsey commanded the Third Fleet.

Task Force 38 undertook air strikes on Okinawa, Formosa, Luzon, and the Visayas in support of the landings on Leyte. The immediate objective was to inflict maximum damage on enemy air, surface, and ground resources and thereby reduce the ability of the enemy to damage U.S. forces during the Leyte landings.

Between 6 and 10 October Task Force 38 attacked Okinawa and the Ryukyu Islands; between 12 and 14 October they attacked Formosa. During the Formosa engagements, the task force was attacked by Japanese aircraft. One attack occurred at night, but using radar-controlled fire, *Iowa* shot one aircraft down with 28 rounds fired in 13 seconds from ten 5-inch guns. At 1515 the next afternoon a flight of three Japanese aircraft being chased by two Hellcat fighters approached the *Iowa*. Two of the Japanese aircraft were destroyed by the Hellcats, but the third aircraft, a Suisei "Judy" dive-bomber, aimed for the *Iowa*'s port beam. It was met by a barrage of 108 rounds of 40-mm shells from five 40-mm quads and 23 rounds of 20-mm from two Oerlikon cannons fired at a range of 1,000 yards. The shells hit the aircraft's engine cowling and the wing, which disintegrated as the aircraft crashed into the sea 300 yards from the port beam. The action of Marine Sergeant John C. Villante, the operator of a 40-mm quad mount, was noted for his constant accurate fire on the Judy aircraft as it was aimed for his area of the ship.

Between 14 and 20 October, Task Force 38 covered the retirement of USS *Canberra* (CA-70) and *Houston*, which had been damaged by torpedoes in actions off Formosa. Task Group 38.1 was then directed to return to Ulithi Atoll to refuel and resupply, but the remainder of the task force took up a position off the east coasts of the major islands of the Philippines on the morning of 24 October in support of the Leyte landings.

The 7,000 islands of the Philippine archipelago presented a 1,000-plus-mile north/south divide separating the South China Sea from the Pacific Ocean. This island structure also represented a link between the Japanese islands to the north and the oil-producing islands to the south. The island of Leyte, part of the Visayas, was exposed to the Pacific Ocean with southeast-facing beaches and uninterrupted lines of communication with U.S. bases, both in the Pacific and New Guinea. It had weakly defended beaches accessible to U.S. forces and offered deep anchorages as well as numerous airfields from which U.S. control over the Philippines might be exerted.

The U.S. advance on the Philippines was a major effort by the U.S. military. It brought together the Central Pacific Drive led by Admiral Nimitz and the advance to the Philippines from New Guinea led by General Douglas MacArthur. By bringing these two drives together, command-and-control of both elements became a major issue. MacArthur's army needed a navy to protect it during its move from New Guinea and related islands to Leyte, and to resupply it with men and material. To this end, the U.S. Seventh Fleet, under the command of Admiral Thomas Kinkaid, reported to General MacArthur, not to Admiral Nimitz. The U.S. Third Fleet under the command of Admiral Halsey reported to Admiral Nimitz in Pearl Harbor.

As part of his full control over his independent command, General MacArthur insisted that Admiral Kinkaid was not to communicate directly with Admiral Halsey but was to route communications through a radio station on Manus Island, part of the Admiralty group, north of New Guinea. This requirement, added to the separate command structure, approved by the president and Admirals King and Nimitz, was to have a significant impact on the effective coordination of naval forces during the forthcoming actions.

The radio station on Manus Island was overwhelmed with the volume of radio messages resulting from the invasion of Leyte. The radio operators stacked the incoming messages and evaluated them as best they could do. However, delays in establishing the correct priority resulted in significant delays in resending urgent messages, with many messages out of sequence.

The Leyte landings took place on 20 October, and U.S. army troops and supplies quickly moved inland. General MacArthur was able to broadcast to the Philippine population that he had returned.

On learning that U.S. forces had landed at Leyte, Admiral Takeo Kurita sailed on 18 October from Lingga Roads, near Singapore, with his First Striking Force of seven battleships: *Yamato, Musashi, Nagato, Kongo, Haruna, Yamashiro,* and *Fuso.* Following refueling in Brunei, Admiral Kurita split his Striking Force into two components, giving Admiral Shoji Nishimura two battleships, *Yamashiro* and *Fuso,* and directing him to approach Leyte Gulf from the south, via the Surigao Strait. With the remaining five battleships, including *Yamato* and *Musashi,* Admiral Kurita approached Leyte Gulf from the north, through the San Bernardino Strait.

Admiral Jisaburō Ozawa and the four remaining Japanese aircraft carriers—*Zuikaku, Zuho, Chitose,* and *Chiyoda*—sailed from the Japanese Inland Sea to appear off the north coast of the Philippines to coincide with the emergence of the Japanese fleet into the Pacific. The movement was intended to entice Admiral Halsey to leave Leyte so that Admirals Kurita and Nishimura could swoop in and attack the troops and transports there.

On 23 October the submarines USS *Dace* (SS-247) and *Darter* (SS-227) on patrol in the Palawan Passage, alerted the U.S. Navy that a large force of Japanese warships was sailing toward the Philippines. After raising the alarm, the submarines then attacked. *Dace* torpedoed and sank the cruiser *Maya*, and *Darter* sank the cruiser *Atago* and severely damaged the cruiser *Takao*.

Now aware of the approach of a significant part of the Japanese fleet, Admiral Halsey ordered an air search to locate the fleet. A reconnaissance plane from USS *Intrepid* in Task Group 38.2 sighted the Japanese fleet on 24 October, but there were no sightings of Japanese aircraft carriers. Task Groups 38.2 and 38.4 attacked both Admiral Kurita and Admiral Nishimura, but the potential prize of battleships *Musashi* and *Yamato* ensured that Admiral Kurita's fleet received most of the carrier fliers' attention. From late morning until late afternoon, *Musashi* was attacked by aircraft from TG 38.2, TG 38.3, and TG 38.4, representing USS

Intrepid, Essex, Lexington, Enterprise, Franklin (CV-13), and *Cabot. Musashi* received an unknown number of torpedoes and bombs and sank late in the afternoon. After the war, the U.S. Naval Technical Mission to Japan estimated that *Musashi* suffered 10 torpedo and 16 bomb hits.

Admiral Kurita reversed the course of his fleet during the afternoon, seeking a respite from Admiral Halsey's air attacks. During this course reversal, search planes from USS *Essex* at 1640 located Admiral Ozawa and the four Japanese carriers that had escaped from Admiral Spruance during the Battle of the Philippine Sea. Admiral Ozawa and his carriers were north of the Philippine's Cape Engaño.

Following Pearl Harbor, the U.S. Navy went through a readjustment of its war strategy in the Pacific. The line of battleships needed to force their way across the Pacific to the Philippines was not available, but aircraft carriers were. The relatively high speed of the carriers and the extended range of their torpedo- and dive-bombers, plus their fighters, demonstrated their considerable striking power. The Battles of the Coral

Third Fleet warships and auxiliaries anchored at Ulithi shortly after the Battle of Leyte Gulf, on 6 November 1944. Battleships *New Jersey* (BB-62) and *Iowa* are at center and right. Five *Essex*-class carriers are moored in line at upper center. (NHHC)

Sea, Midway, Eastern Solomons, Santa Cruz, and Philippine Sea established the aircraft carrier as the primary naval weapon system. To exert command of the sea, aircraft carriers were the mainstay of any naval fleet and critical to naval strategy. Conversely, enemy carriers and not battleships represented the major naval threat to the U.S. Navy and had to be particularly targeted for destruction.

Admiral Nimitz's operating plan to Admiral Halsey for the Third Fleet was to "cover and support forces of the Southwest Pacific in order to assist in the seizure and occupation of objectives in the central Philippines." The Third Fleet was to "destroy enemy naval and air forces in or threatening the Philippines area." At the end of the operating plan was the additional instruction: "In case opportunity for destruction of major portion of the enemy fleet offer or can be created, such destruction becomes primary task." This sentence was seen as necessary to prevent the Third Fleet from becoming tethered to the Leyte beachhead, as had occurred during the invasion of Saipan, with Admiral Mitscher being denied the opportunity to attack the Japanese Fleet on 19 June and the escape of Admiral Ozawa and his aircraft carriers on 21 June.

Accordingly, although Admiral Halsey and his Third Fleet had just sunk the world's largest battleship, the *Musashi*, it remained imperative to attack and sink Admiral Ozawa's four carriers. It is here that the inability of the two admirals, Halsey and Kinkaid, to communicate directly by radio, in accordance with General MacArthur's command-and-control requirement, became critical. The separate chain-of-command and non-coordinated missions also fed into the frustration that followed.

At 1512 on 24 October Admiral Halsey issued his instructions to his task force commanders based on the threat that Admiral Kurita might turn back east, toward the San Bernardino Strait. Halsey's battle plan established Task Force 34, containing battleships USS *Iowa*, *Washington*, and *Alabama*, with *New Jersey* serving as Admiral Halsey's flagship. Admiral Halsey subsequently advised his commanders that if Admiral Kurita did sortie through the San Bernardino Strait, Task Force 34 would be formed when directed by him. Both of these messages—the battle plan and the plan to form Task Force 34—were sent over the Third Fleet and U.S. Navy radio network, not General MacArthur's radio network centered on Manus. However, against

strict instructions not to, Admiral Kinkaid's staff were listening in on Admiral Halsey's messages. This became the crux of the issues that now unfolded.

At 1700 Admiral Ozawa and his carriers were sighted by reconnaissance aircraft east of Cape Engaño, the northernmost tip of the Philippine Islands. Admiral Halsey and his staff reevaluated the unfolding Japanese intentions and timing. They calculated that Admiral Kurita's force could not achieve their original intention of arriving at Leyte Gulf at the same time as Admiral Nishimura. This meant that Admiral Kinkaid had time to defeat Admiral Nishimura and then reposition his battleships and his carrier aircraft to meet Admiral Kurita's ships, which had already been damaged by Third Fleet aircraft.

The air battle of the Philippine Sea had shown that Japanese carrier aircraft had a longer range than U.S. carrier aircraft. In addition, aircraft from Admiral Ozawa's carriers would be able to use 17 Japanese airfields on the island of Luzon to refuel and rearm. To negate these capabilities, Admiral Halsey wanted to use the night to position his fleet much closer to the Japanese carriers. He accordingly ordered his fleet north, rejecting the option to remain off the San Bernardino Strait to avoid attacks by aircraft from both Admiral Ozawa's carriers and the Luzon airfields.

Task Group 38.2, including USS *Iowa*, sailed north at 2000 with Task Groups 38.3 and 38.4. Admiral Halsey's staff initiated radio messages to Admiral Kinkaid that were copied to Admiral King in Washington and to Admiral Nimitz in Pearl Harbor and his Third Fleet commanders. The message stated: "Strike reports indicate enemy force Sibuyan Sea heavily damaged. Am proceeding north with three groups to attack enemy carrier force at dawn."

Shortly after 0235 on 25 October, when Admiral Ozawa's carriers had been located by radar-equipped Hellcats, Admiral Halsey ordered Task Force 34 to be formed and to sail ahead of the carriers in preparation for battle with the Japanese carriers. This tactical move was identical to the positioning of Admiral Lee and Task Group 58.7 in the Battle of the Philippine Sea.

At 0648 Admiral Halsey received a radio message from Admiral Kinkaid, on board USS *Wasatch* (AGC-9), an amphibious command ship, stating that Seventh Fleet surface forces were engaging enemy surface forces in Surigao Strait. In addition, Admiral Kinkaid asked whether Task Force 34 was guarding San Bernardino

Strait. Admiral Halsey replied, "Negative. Task Force 34 is with carrier groups now engaging enemy carrier force."

The message from Kinkaid had been sent at 0412. The intervening time of 2 hours and 36 minutes was a result of delays in processing the message through the Manus radio station, in accordance with General MacArthur's orders, although the radio system on board *Wasatch* was more than powerful enough to have transmitted messages directly to Admiral Halsey on board USS *New Jersey*.

At 0802 Halsey received a further message from Kinkaid that "enemy surface vessels Surigao Strait retiring, pursued by our light forces." This message had originally been transmitted at 0623, with Manus taking 1 hour and 39 minutes to route the message to Halsey. A flurry of messages then followed, mainly in plain language that Taffy 3, a force of six escort carriers, was being shelled by battleships. A request from Kinkaid that fast battleships were needed at Leyte Gulf made no sense given Halsey's earlier message stating the fast battleships were engaging the enemy. However, Halsey ordered Admiral John "Slew" McCain, commander of Task Group 38.1, which was refueling, to sail at "best possible speed" to strike the enemy force northeast of Leyte Gulf. Kinkaid sent further messages in plain language informing that his battleships were short of ammunition and requesting immediate support for his escort carriers. Halsey responded by confirming that Task Group 38.1 was ordered to assist Kinkaid immediately.

At 0850 Admiral Halsey was advised by his carrier strike force that they had sunk one aircraft carrier of Admiral Ozawa's force, and that two more carriers were badly hit. A second carrier strike against Admiral Ozawa had been launched. Admiral Halsey ordered Task Force 34, with USS *Iowa*, to increase speed to catch up with Admiral Ozawa's now-depleted force and complete its destruction. Admiral Halsey calculated that Task Force 34 would reach Admiral Ozawa by noon.

Admiral Nimitz radioed Halsey at 1000, with the question, "Where is Task Force 34?" Unfortunately, the message was lengthened in transmission so that it read, "Where is (Repeat), Where is Task Group 34?" Additionally, padding that was added to messages to confuse enemy decoding—in this case reading "The world wonders"—was physically left on the message to be read by Halsey. The garbled message thus produced an emotional response, as Halsey interpreted it as a major rebuke to him. Later Halsey was advised of the errors made in transmission and decoding padding.

At 1100 Admiral Halsey ordered Task Group 34 to reverse course and sail to the San Bernardino Strait. *Iowa* and *New Jersey* therefore sailed south, with three cruisers and a destroyer screen. At 2340 *Iowa* went to General Quarters. At 0044 on 26 October a single surface target was picked up on the SG radar at 33,000 yards, and at 0045 the target was picked up at 32,000 yards by the Mark 8 radar in the forward main director. The cruisers and destroyers were ordered forward to attack the target, a destroyer identified as *Nowaki*, which was then set ablaze from bow to stern by torpedoes and sustained gunfire. It sank at 0136. *Nowaki* had previously escaped from *Iowa* at Truk.

Meanwhile, Task Groups 38.3 and 38.4 commanded by Admiral Mitscher had continued north as directed by Admiral Halsey. On 25 October they launched additional air strikes against Admiral Ozawa's force. All four carriers were sunk, together with a cruiser and destroyer. The sinking of these 4 aircraft carriers left Japan with only 3 carriers out of a fleet of 21 carriers that Japan operated during the war. Admiral Halsey had amply satisfied Admiral Nimitz's directive that, "in case opportunity for destruction of major portion of the enemy fleet offer or can be created, such destruction becomes primary task." Two of the remaining three carriers, *Shinano* and *Shinyo*, were sunk by U.S. submarines during November. The two battleships *Ise* and *Hyuga* were damaged but were able to return to Japan.

Admiral Kurita had brought his fleet through the San Bernardino Strait into the Pacific and steered south toward Leyte. With his fleet of four battleships and eight cruisers, he encountered an escort carrier unit, Taffy 3, comprising six escort carriers and four destroyers. The destroyers attacked the Japanese fleet with such aggression that, combined with the attacking U.S. carrier aircraft from escort carriers, convinced Admiral Kurita he was advancing toward a major carrier task force, so he withdrew to the north and passed back through the San Bernardino Strait. As a result, *Iowa* and *New Jersey*, with three cruisers and a destroyer screen, did not encounter Admiral Kurita and his fleet.

KAMIKAZE RAIDS

The battle for Leyte saw the Japanese introduce kamikaze raids against U.S. aircraft carriers. The USS *Iowa* remained in the east of Philippine waters as the Third Fleet continued to provide air cover to the U.S. Army as it fought its way across Leyte Island. On 25 November, *Iowa* was 75 miles east of Luzon as part of Task Group 38.2. *Iowa*'s radar system enabled *Iowa* to locate Japanese aircraft at a range of 40 miles and thereby give sufficient warning for the antiaircraft batteries to be manned. At closer ranges, the sky directors had to be aware of accompanying destroyers fouling the range and the risk of friendly fire. The accompanying three aircraft carriers, *Intrepid*, *Cabot*, and *Hancock*, were subject to kamikaze attacks. *Iowa*'s AA control spotted three Japanese aircraft approaching low on the water from astern. The *Iowa* had the entire 5-inch/38-caliber battery assigned to the aft director, Sky 4. But the aft port 5-inch mounts could only open fire when the aircraft reached a range of 6,500 yards, and the 5-inch guns could train out of their danger sectors. *Iowa* fired Mark 32 fuzed shells, and Mount 10 scored a direct hit on the leading aircraft. The rangefinder operator of Sky 4 reported that the aircraft disintegrated, with a propeller and radial engine flying through the air without an attached plane. The second attacking aircraft flew along the port quarter of *Iowa* toward *Intrepid*, in range

of both 20-mm and 40-mm guns and was shot down in flames. The third aircraft suddenly climbed several hundred feet and, despite being hit multiple times by 20-mm guns, dove on the flight deck of *Intrepid*.

A few minutes later a single Japanese aircraft at 6,000 feet flew along the fore and aft line of *Iowa* and 13 quad mounts of 40-mm and 35 20-mm guns scored hits, with the aircraft crashing 100 yards off *Iowa*'s starboard bow requiring the 20-mm bow gunners to quickly retire aft. *Iowa* fired on several other attacking aircraft but could not prevent them from crashing on board *Intrepid* and *Cabot*. The *Intrepid* suffered 65 casualties and significant damage and had to retire to the United States for repairs.

In addition to protecting the aircraft carriers with antiaircraft fire, *Iowa* carried out rescue missions to pick up their downed air crew who had had to parachute from their aircraft, landing in the sea. *Iowa*'s float Kingfisher aircraft, launched along the catapult on the aft deck, carried out multiple missions to pick up downed pilots and help return them to their ship.

During all the steaming USS *Iowa* had completed, a vibration on the No. 3 shaft had been noted when the ship reached and exceeded 25 knots. The problem was thought to be the bearings in the strut housing the propeller shaft; however, the ship was able to maintain its station with the Fleet.

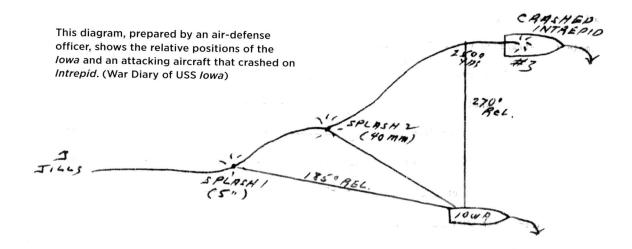

This diagram, prepared by an air-defense officer, shows the relative positions of the *Iowa* and an attacking aircraft that crashed on *Intrepid*. (War Diary of USS *Iowa*)

DISTRIBUTION:
CINCPAC VIA 'CHAIN OF COMMAND (ORIG. & ?.)
COMINCH (Readiness) (1)
COMBATPAC (1).

USS *Iowa* at sea with Task Force 38 in December 1944. Photographed by LCDR Charles Fenno Jacobs, USNR. (NARA)

REPAIRS AND UPGRADES

After the prolonged actions in the Philippine Sea and at Leyte Gulf, the Third Fleet had a well-deserved ten-day rest in the Ulithi Atoll anchorage in early December. The rest, relaxation, and resupply were a welcome change from the constant attention to duty and awareness of imminent danger. Then, on 11 December 1944, *Iowa* sailed from Ulithi with the Third Fleet to provide air cover for the invasion of the Philippine island of Mindoro. During the invasion the Third Fleet prevented Japanese aircraft from taking off from the airfields located on the major island of Luzon, where they also destroyed nearly 200 aircraft on the ground. On 17

December the Third Fleet retired toward Ulithi to refuel and steamed into a typhoon that sank three destroyers, with the loss of 790 men and significant damage to most of the ships, including *Iowa*. At Ulithi, the fleet repaired damage and made good on aircraft, ship's boats, and other items that had been lost to the typhoon. For *Iowa*, the damage was significant. The troubled third propeller shaft had dropped three inches in its strut bearing and caused heavy vibration and knocking, particularly when the ship reached and exceeded 25 knots.

The problem was thought to be the bearings in the strut that housed the propeller shaft. The engineers at

USS *Iowa* in floating dry dock ABSD-2 for temporary repairs to her propeller, Seeadler Harbor, Manus, Admiralty Islands, 24 December 1944. (NARA)

Ulithi locked the shaft and immobilized the engine so the ship could continue to sail on the remaining three operative propellers. *Iowa* then sailed to the island of Manus where, on 27 December, she was dry-docked in the Advance Base Sectional Dock, No. 2 (ABSD-2), located in Port Seeadler. This floating dry dock was part of the U.S. Navy's answer to the lack of Pacific Ocean bases west of Pearl Harbor. The ten separate sections of the dry dock had been built in Mare Island, California, and towed to Manus. The ABSD-2 could accommodate battleships and aircraft carriers as its ten sections, when joined together, were 927 feet long and 133 feet wide. The lifting capacity of the dry dock was close to 100,000 tons. The ABSD-2 also comprised a power plant and a 15-ton crane and could undertake significant ship repairs either to return warships to service or to enable them to return to the United States.

In the ABSD-2 dry dock, *Iowa's* No. 3 propeller was removed and the extent of the damage to the propeller shaft was seen and identified. With the propeller lashed down on the aft deck, *Iowa* sailed to the San Francisco Navy Yard at Hunters Point, arriving on 16 January 1945.

USS *Iowa* spent 16 January to 18 March at Hunters Point. Beyond repairing the No. 3 propeller shaft and reattaching the propeller, a series of changes were made to the superstructure. The navigating bridge was fully enclosed with windshields across the front and along the sides of the pilothouse. Above the navigating bridge, a platform was installed around the front of the conning tower. A new foremast was installed with a new SU target-acquisition surface-search radar antenna housed in a radome atop the topmast. The mainmast was strengthened with stronger supporting struts, and the topmast carried the aft SG surface-search antenna. An SR long-range air-search antenna was also added to the maintop. The ship's aircraft were updated with three Curtiss SC-1 Seahawk scout planes replacing the Kingfisher aircraft.

USS *Iowa* inside floating dry dock ABSD-2 for temporary repairs, Seeadler Harbor, Manus, Admiralty Islands, 24 December 1944. (NARA)

USS *Iowa* in Dry Dock No. 4 looking northeast (1945), Hunters Point Naval Shipyard, Dry Dock No. 4, East Terminus of Palou Avenue, San Francisco, San Francisco County, California. (Library of Congress)

OKINAWA AND THE MAIN JAPANESE ISLANDS

On 19 March 1945 USS *Iowa* sailed from San Francisco for Okinawa to relieve USS *New Jersey*. It arrived on station on 15 April, near the beginning of the U.S. Army and Marine invasion of Okinawa, which began on 1 April. The battle for Okinawa raged for 82 days, until 22 June.

Okinawa was a critical island for the U.S. Pacific strategy. Its proximity to Japan offered a fleet anchorage, bases for troops, and the Kadena Air Base, which could be used to stage troops, aircraft, and equipment for the invasion of Japan, planned for November 1945.

However, this proximity carried a high cost as Okinawa was within range of kamikaze aircraft flying from the southernmost of the main Japanese islands, Kyushu. In the waters surrounding Okinawa, kamikaze aircraft sank 12 U.S. destroyers, 15 amphibious warfare ships, and 9 other ships. Besides the kamikaze aircraft, the Japanese navy sailed the *Yamato*, their last major battleship, on a suicide mission to sink as many ships as possible and then beach itself on Okinawa and use its guns in support of the Japanese army garrison. When the *Yamato* was sighted by carrier aircraft, Task Groups 58.1, 58.3, and 58.4 launched 227 aircraft in three waves. The torpedo bombers concentrated their attack on the *Yamato*'s port beam to prevent the ship's damage control from trying to maintain an even keel by counterflooding the opposite side to torpedo damage. In addition to sinking the *Yamato*, the aircraft also sank the cruiser *Yahagi* and four destroyers. Like the *Musashi*, the *Yamato* was sunk by multiple torpedoes, estimated at between 9 and 12, with possibly 7 bomb hits. *Yamato* went down in the East China Sea, 200 miles northwest of Okinawa.

Following a resupply break in Leyte Gulf, *Iowa* turned toward Japan. The Japanese air force had been severely diminished, and the fast battleships with *Iowa* were able to bombard the main Japanese islands of Hokkaido and Honshu. On 14–15 July the steel mills at Muroran, on Hokkaido, were bombarded by *Iowa*, *Missouri*, and *Wisconsin*. *Iowa* fired 133 16-inch shells at the Japan Steel Works, where naval armaments were produced, and 139 shells at the Wanishi Iron Works, where coke and pig iron were produced. *Iowa* fired at ranges of 28,000 to 30,000 yards between 0936 and 1030. The three fast battleships fired 428 shells in total at the Japan Steel Works, with only 63 hits landing within the boundaries of the plant. Visibility was hampered by a low cloud base at 1,500 feet and by the smoke and dust from the multiple explosions. Air spot was undertaken by carrier aircraft rather than the battleship's Seahawk scout planes.

On 17–18 July the fast battleships bombarded Hitachi, on Honshu. The Hitachi area contained a large number of industrial plants, including a copper refinery, multiple engineering works, an arms factory, and other industrial activities. The fast battleships deployed for this mission included USS *Iowa*, *Missouri*, *Wisconsin*, *North Carolina*, and *Alabama*. HMS *King George V*, the flagship of the British Pacific Fleet, joined the U.S. battleships but had a different target allocation, which were the Densen engineering plant and the Taga engineering works. The bombardment took place at night, commencing at 1110 and ending at 0110. Ranges were between 23,000 and 35,000 yards and targets were spotted by radar and LORAN. *Iowa* and her fellow battleships fired 1,238 16-inch shells, and HMS *King George V* fired 267 14-inch shells. Subsequent air reconnaissance and photography showed that few targets were hit, and those that were had only limited damage.

To improve bombardment accuracy, *Iowa* sailed to Hawai'i to practice shelling at the bombing range on the island of Kahoolawe, on 29–30 July. Radio-controlled drones were brought on board and then flown to provide more realistic antiaircraft exercises in place of towed sleeves.

The ship then returned to Japanese waters to rejoin the fleet. During this occasion *Iowa* missed sailing with the Third Fleet while its aircraft sank the battleship *Haruna* at anchor at Kure.

5 March 1945 after USS *Iowa*'s last wartime overhaul. She just received the new enclosed bridge and some new electronics and now carried SC-1 Seahawk aircraft. (NARA)

JAPANESE SURRENDER

The USS *Missouri* (BB-63), escorted by the USS *Nicholas* (DD-449) and followed by the USS *Iowa*, steams up Tokyo Bay, 29 August 1945. This photograph was flown to Washington, D.C., directly from Japan, arriving on 2 September 1945, the day the Japanese surrender was signed. (NHHC)

In the early morning of 15 August, *Iowa* and the Fleet received the news that President Harry Truman had accepted the Japanese government's offer of unconditional surrender. On 27 August *Iowa* and *Missouri* sailed into Sagami Bay to take the surrender of the Yokosuka naval district and base and to prepare for the surrender ceremony scheduled for 2 September. On dropping anchor in Sagami Bay, *Iowa*'s pit log showed that she had sailed 190,313 steaming miles since commissioning.

On 28 August the two battleships left Sagami Bay and sailed the few miles into Tokyo Bay, where they headed for Yokohama to provide the setting for the surrender ceremony. As they sailed into Tokyo Bay, they passed the Yokosuka naval base and the Japanese battleship *Mikasa*, which had been Admiral Tōgō Heihachirō's flagship when defeating the Imperial Russian Navy in the Battle of Tsushima in 1905. The *Mikasa* had symbolized the emergence of Japan as a major naval power. The entry of *Iowa* and *Missouri* into Tokyo Bay and past *Mikasa* provided a clear end of Japanese naval power during World War II.

USS *Iowa* served as the radio communications center to the U.S. and Allied powers during the preparation for the formal surrender and during the ceremony itself on board USS *Missouri*. The *Iowa* returned to the United States on 20 September 1945 as part of the Magic Carpet operation of returning home to the United States numbers of U.S. servicemen as well as U.S. prisoners of war who had been held in Japan.

MISSED OPPORTUNITIES

With the war over and USS *Iowa* back in home waters, it is worth recalling that this ship had been designed and ordered with its primary purpose to fight enemy battleships, hence the nine 16-inch/50-caliber guns, heavy armor, and supporting fire-control equipment. Only two opportunities occurred during the war where such a battle could have happened for USS *Iowa*, but the opportunities passed.

The first missed opportunity occurred during the battle of the Philippine Sea, when Admiral Mitscher, commander of the Task Forces, asked Admiral Willis Augustus Lee, commander of the battleships in Task Force 7, "Do you desire night engagement? It may be we can make air contact late this afternoon and attack tonight. Otherwise, we should retire eastward tonight." On Monday morning of 18 June 1944, the Japanese Mobile Fleet and the U.S. Task Force 58 were 600-plus miles apart, and Admiral Mitscher was planning a rapid advance westward of his Task Force to bring the Mobile Fleet within the range of his carrier aircraft. If a battle had occurred, Admiral Mitscher was considering that the battleships, with their speed, radar, and heavy armament of 16-inch guns, could finish off wounded Japanese carriers and battleships in a night action.

Admiral Lee had fought and won a night action against the Japanese battleship *Kirishima*, several Japanese cruisers, and destroyers in the restricted waters off Guadalcanal. Admiral Lee's knowledge and use of radar in night action was a key determinant in his success. However, Admiral Lee replied to Admiral Mitscher, "Do not (repeat not) believe we should seek night engagement. Possible advantages of radar more than offset by difficulties of communications and lack of training in fleet tactics at night. Would press pursuit of damaged or fleeing enemy however at any time."

Admiral Lee's reply reflected his experience of night actions. Even with radar, Admiral Lee in USS *Washington* had not known whether USS *South Dakota* was still following in its assigned position. This had caused Admiral Lee to hold off firing at *Kirishima* in case it was USS *South Dakota*, until he had firm knowledge of USS *South Dakota*'s location. Additionally, Admiral Lee had the knowledge from the night battles of Savo and Guadalcanal that the Japanese navy was highly efficient in night battles. Admiral Lee's last comment in his reply to Admiral Mitscher—"and lack of training

in fleet tactics at night"—also reflected that the focus of the fast battleships on supporting aircraft carriers had minimized opportunities to train as a battleship line of battle and maneuver as a fleet. The potential clash of the two fleets at night suggested the possibility of a melee battle with significant confusion as well as a high risk of battle damage from Japanese torpedoes.

The second opportunity occurred during the Battle of Leyte Gulf, with the battleships sailing north with Admiral Halsey, rather than standing guard off the San Bernardino Strait to meet the Japanese fleet as it emerged into the Pacific. The strategic need to destroy Japanese aircraft carriers and thereby limit Japanese aircraft to land-based airfields was seen as paramount, as expressed by Admiral Nimitz and agreed by Admiral Halsey.

But this raises the unanswerable question as to which battleship would have survived victoriously if the USS *Iowa* had met the *Yamato*. Given the demise of both *Musashi* and *Yamato* by carrier-based aircraft, the only way USS *Iowa* and *Yamato* could meet for battle would be at night. Putting escorting cruisers and destroyers to the side, combat would be radar driven with a clear advantage going to USS *Iowa*. However, a lucky shot from *Yamato* hitting near the base of the fire-control tower would disrupt many of the connections between radar and the plotting room disrupting gunfire until secondary backup systems came into effect.

The sinking of *Musashi* and *Yamato* by carrier aircraft indicated they were able to absorb damage by bombs, but multiple torpedo hits were the reason they sank. A prolonged bombardment by 16-inch heavy shells may not be sufficient to sink *Yamato* unless, like *Bismarck* and HMS *Hood*, a shell and or its explosive force reached a magazine, or unless, like *Bismarck*, battered by 16-inch armor-piercing shells fired by HMS *Rodney*, USS *Iowa* called in an accompanying cruiser to deliver a volley of torpedoes to finally sink *Yamato*.

The Pacific war represented significant frustration for battleship crews, with only *Kirishima*, *Yamashiro*, and *Fuso* sunk in battles with U.S. battleships. The marrying of 16-inch guns with Ford rangekeepers and radar clearly demonstrated their capability. USS *Iowa* was teased as the mast top of *Nowaki*, ranged by radar at 39,000 yards, slipped below the horizon.

A further irony of the Pacific war reflected that the strategy for the Japanese navy was the "decisive battleship battle" into which they poured significant resources, including the construction of *Musashi* and *Yamato*. The decisive battle occurred off the coast of Samar, when Admiral Kurita on board *Yamato*, with battleships *Nagato*, *Kongo*, and *Haruna* with him, battled the USS *Heermann* (DD-532), *Samuel B. Robert* (DD-823), *Johnston* (DD-557), and *Hoel* (DD-533) destroyers and destroyer escorts guarding Taffy 3, comprising six escort carriers. The two-hour battle resulted in the loss of the three destroyers and destroyer escorts of the guarding ships and the escort carrier USS *Gambier Bay* (CVE-73), but Admiral Kurita turned his fleet of four battleships away and retired north. Perhaps the best epitaph for the "decisive battleship battle" was the comment by a Taffy 3 sailor, "Damn it, boys, they're getting away!"

KOREA

On 24 March 1949 USS *Iowa* was put into the reserve fleet, held in San Francisco. It remained there until 25 August 1951, when she was recommissioned in preparation for service in the Korean War. In March 1952 *Iowa* sailed from the West Coast for Korea, where she relieved the USS *Wisconsin*. On 31 March 1952 the two battleships met each other at Yokosuka, Japan, now a major U.S. naval base.

In Korea on 8 April 1952, *Iowa* opened fire with her 16-inch/50-caliber guns on the North Korean railway system near Chaho. This strike blocked railway tunnels and brought large landslides down on the railway track. The following day she sailed south to support South Korean troops in their battle with North Korean army units.

Following at-sea resupply, *Iowa* supported the U.S. X Corps by firing at a range of 18 miles to destroy enemy command posts, bunkers, and mortar positions. X Corps reported that enemy action against them was stopped by this bombardment.

USS *Iowa* bombarding communist positions off northern Korea, 10 September 1952. (NavSource, U.S. Navy)

Off Koje, Korea, firing her 16-in guns at enemy coastal defenses. (NHHC)

A key feature of naval gunfire was that it could be used against reverse-slope enemy positions that could not be reached by army artillery fire. Naval ships could sail north of the battle line and then fire back on enemy positions.

USS *Iowa* took part in multiple gun strikes against North Korean transport sites, mainly rail tunnels and railroads. On 25 May she bombarded Chongjin as part of a joint action with four 50-plane carrier strikes. *Iowa* stayed on the bombardment line for 11 hours sailing at 10 knots up and down the coast while firing 202 rounds of 16-inch shells. She destroyed a railway roundhouse, an iron works, and a textile factory. One shell hit a gas storage facility with a resultant vast explosion and then started a major fire at a shipyard. Two gantry cranes were destroyed and three others were damaged. A power station and three transformers were also destroyed.

U.S. ships engaged in shore bombardment had the following objectives:

- Gunfire in support of the ground forces on the flanks of the battle line.

- Interruption of the enemy's coastal rail and road network in coordination with air-, carrier-, and ground-based efforts.

- Prevention of rebuilding damaged and broken bridges.

- Destruction of enemy anti-invasion defenses.

- Harassment of major North Korean ports and railway transport centers.

- Gunfire support for minesweepers.

- Participation in amphibious operations.

- Flack suppression in support of air strikes.

In one operation in the Songin-Chaho area on 27 May 1952, *Iowa* fired 98 rounds of 16-inch shells, demolishing five bridges, sealing four tunnel entrances, and tearing up railway track, undermining track bed,

USS *Iowa* fires her 16-in/50-cal guns at targets in North Korea, circa April–October 1952. (NHHC)

and covering railway track by causing landslides of earth and rock from hillsides.

The accuracy of *Iowa*'s gunfire was high. U.S. troops could call down gunfire as close as 300 yards to their positions. The *Iowa*'s accuracy was a result of detailed planning with precise navigation and shiphandling plus clear spotting instructions by the ship's helicopters, air spotting by supporting carrier aircraft, and spotters ashore with Army and Marine troops.

Communications between the ship and the spotters took a lot of adjustment to align the differing equipment and methodologies. If a spotter was flying a carrier aircraft, spotting was quite complicated. Setup had to be done by radio before the spotter left the carrier. Once in the air, the pilot had to manage his aircraft, locate the target, communicate the results of the ship's gunfire, and advise corrections for the next salvo.

Ground spotters with the Army provided a more accurate assessment of gunfire accuracy. However, communication to the ship by differing radio systems and networks required the ship to use portable radio equipment to access the frequencies being used. As the portable equipment could not be operated directly from locations within the ship's gunnery organization, in particular the main battery plot, delays and makeup interfaces often hindered gunfire accuracy.

Although enemy flak could pose a hazard for helicopters, by far the best system for spotting was the ship's own helicopter and crew. With on-ship training and crew interface, communication between the ship and helicopter was highly effective. Another advantage of the ship's helicopter was the ability to fly well within enemy territory to rescue downed pilots. In July 1952 the *Lucky Lady*, a helicopter piloted by Lieutenant Robert L. Dolton, flew 35 miles northwest of Hungnam to rescue the pilot of a downed Vought F4U Corsair carrier fighter. The pilot was being actively hunted by North Korean troops. Dalton was able to locate the pilot on the side of a steep hill. He placed the nose wheel of the helicopter on the ground but with the body and tail structure off the ground. Marine W. A. Meyer fired his semiautomatic rifle from the door of the helicopter to keep enemy troops away, enabling Lieutenant H. A. Reidl to reach the helicopter and be returned safely to his ship, USS *Princeton*. Dolton was awarded the Distinguished Flying Cross, and Meyer received the Naval Air Medal for the successful completion of this high-risk operation.

On 25 September 1952 USS *Iowa*, working with the Royal Navy destroyer HMS *Charity*, caught a North Korean train in the open on a coastal railway line and fired 45 rounds of 16-inch shells at the locomotive and the 30 boxcars it was pulling. The train was obliterated.

Iowa's gunfire was interrupted on two occasions by problems in turret 2. When the ship was recommissioned, the draft of sailors allocated to *Iowa* lacked experience with 16-inch-gun turret operations. To be ready to sail on schedule, the Navy transferred sailors to the ship who had experience and training with heavy-cruiser gun turrets. While this worked as demonstrated by the volume and accuracy of 16-inch gunfire from *Iowa*, two mishaps did occur. Early in April 1952, shortly after the ship entered the gun line and was firing on the Toejo-Sinpo area, the center powder car for turret 2 dumped three bags of powder while hoisting them, which jammed the top of the hoist. The malfunction was caused by the lower powder-hoist operator's failure to secure the powder tray dumping handle. The center gun was out of action until the hoist could be safely cleared, which took several hours. Near the end of *Iowa*'s time on the gun line, the left gun in turret 2 suffered a broken hydraulic line, which required several hours to fix.

The 40-mm, World War II–vintage Bofor antiaircraft guns on board *Iowa* were becoming increasingly unreliable. In August 1952 water entered the electrical motors and controllers of 15 of the 19 Bofor guns, shorting out the guns' electrical system and making the 15 guns inoperable until they were repaired. As important, jet fighters were too fast for the old Bofor systems. The U.S. Navy had developed a heavier 3-inch antiaircraft gun to defend against jet fighters, but it was not available for the *Iowa*-class battleships. As the Bofors did not offer reliable air defense, *Iowa* recommended that U.S. Navy ships receive continuous air cover when operating as far north as Chongjin, 48 miles from the China and Soviet borders.

The *Iowa*'s last Korean operation involved a deception feint offshore Kojo. The plan was to create the impression that an amphibious landing was about to take place on 14 October 1952. Together with the heavy cruiser USS *Toledo* (CA-133), *Iowa* laid down a heavy preinvasion barrage, hoping North Korean troops would withdraw from their frontline defensive positions and rush to Kojo to repel invading troops. If

Port bow view of battleship USS *Iowa* passing through the Gaillard Cut as it transits the Panama Canal. (NARA)

A view of the USS *Iowa* passing through the Pedro Miguel Locks. (NARA)

this occurred, the arriving troops at Kojo would then be hit both by shelling from the two ships and by bombs from attacking carrier aircraft. The deception was not successful as the North Korean response was insignificant. *Iowa*'s helicopter was used to recover a downed pilot from the carrier USS *Bon Homme Richard* (CV-31) who had parachuted into the sea off Kojo.

During her six-month duty off the coast of Korea, USS *Iowa* completed 40 gun strikes on coastal transportation facilities, trains, supply and ammunition areas, gun emplacements, bridges, power stations, and troop concentrations. The gun strikes used 4,000 16-inch and 8,000 5-inch shells. In addition, and demonstrating her storage capability, *Iowa* refueled 12 destroyers with 720,000 gallons of fuel.

USS *Iowa* sails under the Bridge of the Americas into the Pacific Ocean. (NARA)

An aerial view of USS *Iowa* in Dry Dock No. 4. (NARA)

After stopping again at Yokosuka, *Iowa* sailed for Norfolk on 19 October 1952, where she was overhauled. *Iowa* then took on board midshipmen from the Naval Academy and departed for the Caribbean for training exercises. She served as the flagship for the Second Fleet during Operation Mariner, which was a set of NATO naval exercises in support of convoys to Europe from the United States. NATO had been formed on 4 April 1949 as a collective defense against aggression from the Soviet Union. The exercises involved nine navies and lasted for 19 days in July 1953. The ships had to contend with atrocious Atlantic weather, which posed a challenging complement to the *Iowa*'s experiences with Pacific typhoons.

USS *Iowa* again took on midshipmen for their training cruise the following year. In a unique event off Guantánamo Bay, Cuba, *Iowa* joined her three sister ships of the *Iowa* class, USS *New Jersey*, *Missouri*, and *Wisconsin*. This would be the only time these four battleships operated together.

In January 1955 *Iowa* entered the Mediterranean Sea at Gibraltar and passed Oran, Naples, Istanbul, and Athens. This exercise of U.S. naval might was intended to demonstrate to the Soviet Union that the

Crew on USS *Iowa* work to move 16-in projectiles brought on board from a barge. (NARA)

UNITED STATES NAVAL INSTITUTE

U.S. Navy could operate with allies close to the Soviets' southern borders. After returning to the United States in December, the *Iowa* was rearmed with nine new 16-inch/50-caliber guns. The replaced guns had fired 8,279 rounds since first being installed in August 1942.

As part of the massive nuclear-retaliation defense plan of the United States, in 1956 the *Iowa* was modified to carry nine nuclear 16-inch shells in its turret 2 barbette. If ever used, this weapon, referred to as Mark 23, would yield a 20-kiloton blast.

In June 1957 the *Iowa* took part in the International Naval Review off Hampton Roads. During this review,

a Piasecki HUP helicopter landed on USS *Iowa*'s No. 1 16-inch gun turret to demonstrate the helicopter's capability. Boeing subsequently bought the helicopter's manufacturer.

In September 1957 *Iowa* took part in Operation Strike Back. This was a further NATO naval exercise to test the allies' response to a hypothetical Soviet Union attack. The NATO fleet comprised two battleships, the *Iowa* and the *Wisconsin*, as well as nine aircraft carriers and 189 other ships. This was the first naval exercise in which two nuclear-propelled submarines took part, USS *Nautilus* (SSN-571) and *Seawolf* (SSN-575).

A crew member prepares to lower a 16-in projectile into a magazine on USS *Iowa*. (NARA)

QM1 Ronald Schultz operates the helm of USS *Iowa*. (NARA)

(right) USS *Iowa* fires a broadside to starboard from its Mk 7 16-in guns. (NARA)

(middle) Battleship Division 2 in line abreast formation 7 June 1954 in the Virginia Capes operating area on the only occasion that all four *Iowa*-class battleships were photographed operating together. The ship closest to the camera is USS *Iowa*. The others are (from near to far): USS *Wisconsin* (BB-64), USS *Missouri* (BB-63), and USS *New Jersey* (BB-62). (NHHC)

(bottom) An elevated port view of USS *Iowa* during the International Naval Review. (NARA)

NEW ROLES FOR BATTLESHIPS

USS *Iowa* sailed to the Philadelphia Navy Yard and was decommissioned and deactivated on 24 February 1958. The deactivation process took several months to implement. It involved ensuring that internal humidity did not exceed 40 percent, which was achieved by closing all openings, except one, to the outside environment and installing large dehumidifiers. Most radar and communications equipment was removed for storage ashore. Gun turrets were sealed and the guns packed with grease. Cathodic protection was added to the hull to protect against electrolysis. The ship was inspected on an ongoing basis by Reserve Fleet personnel and monitored for any flooding of bilges and other spaces below the waterline spaces.

When *Iowa* was examined in 1982 in preparation for reactivation, the ship was found to be in excellent condition. Over those 24 years that *Iowa* had been in mothballs, the question of what to do with the old battleships had been debated. Proposals ranged from scrapping them, as embodiments of obsolete naval warfare technologies, to modernizing them with batteries of missiles to accommodate new roles. Each suggestion foundered on budget considerations, given the modern Navy's focus on nuclear-powered aircraft carriers and Poseidon missile–carrying nuclear submarines.

As the debates in the United States continued, the Soviet Navy became larger and stronger. By 1964 the Soviet navy had developed a blue-water capability with ships, submarines, and naval aircraft. By the late 1970s the Soviets had 1,700 ships in service compared to 479 ships of the U.S. Navy. The Soviet nuclear-powered guided missile armed *Kirov*-class battlecruisers had no counterpart in the U.S. Navy. These *Kirov* ships were seen as a major threat to U.S. carrier task forces. This changing strategic environment and the focus on nuclear-powered carriers and missile-carrying submarines caused a reevaluation of the needs of the U.S. Navy to maintain its command of the seas.

A key ingredient in the reevaluation was a paper by Charles Myers titled "A Sea-Based Interdiction System for Power Projection" and published in U.S. Naval Institute *Proceedings*. Myers, an ex-carrier pilot, suggested that naval aircraft were not capable of providing and sustaining adequate firepower to support land invasions or withdrawals. Relieving carrier aircraft of their land-attack mission obligations would permit them to concentrate on their better uses, which are to protect U.S. naval forces from enemy aircraft and submarines.

A starboard quarter view of the Soviet Krivak I class frigate *Zharkyy* operating near USS *Iowa*. (NARA)

In contrast, sea-based land bombardment would best be conducted by interdiction/assault ships, with "interdiction" referring to bombardment by a ship's big guns and "assault" referring to troop transport to beaches. The most cost-effective way to create a first wave of interdiction/assault ships would be to repurpose the four mothballed *Iowa*-class battleships. Three of the ships would be purposed for interdiction and the fourth for assault. During overhaul, certain guns could be replaced either by other guns or by missile-firing capabilities. The ships could operate in fairly shallow waters, relatively immune from submarine attacks. Defensively, the armor of the battleships made them already "the most survivable ship ever developed." Myers estimated that the most recently overhauled battleship, the *New Jersey*, could

be readied to operational status in six months at a cost of $30 million.

The Myers article fed into the national debate on military preparedness prior to the November 1980 federal election. Ronald Reagan was elected president on a platform that included a restoration of military strength. Reagan brought into his administration John Lehman as Secretary of the Navy. Lehman's enthusiasm for a reenergized U.S. Navy led to a revised naval strategy based on maritime technological and ship-design superiority. A goal was set of rebuilding the Navy to a strength of 600 warships. This new and invigorated strategy had echoes of Theodore Roosevelt and his advice to "carry a big stick."

To achieve that number of ships, shipbuilding and reactivation of reserve ships became important priorities.

In this context the *Iowa*-class battleships were an important component. On 1 September 1982 the *Iowa* was towed from the Philadelphia Navy Yard to Avondale Shipyard in New Orleans to undergo the first stage of her modernization.

While the enemy battleships *Bismarck*, *Musashi*, and *Yamato* had been sunk during World War II, they all had taken massive amounts of gun, bomb, and torpedo hits before they sank. Plus, these enemy battleships had been operating without air cover. With those examples in mind, strong weight was given to the armor protection for the reactivated *Iowa*-class battleships, and to the multiple watertight compartments that inhibited the spread of damage from hits by enemy projectiles and thus helped preserve buoyancy.

A BGM-109 Tomahawk cruise missile is launched from USS *Iowa* in the Gulf of Mexico during a firing test on the Eglin Air Force Base range. (NARA)

Additionally, the integrated pumping system could dewater flooded compartments, and the firefighting facilities were substantial.

The tasks envisaged for the modernized *Iowa*-class battleships were to

- Sail into the highest-threat seaways with carrier task forces;

- Sail into lower-threat seaways without carrier air cover but backed by supporting escorts;

- Support amphibious landings;

- Undertake offensive operations against surface and shore targets;

- Provide close-in defense against aircraft and anti-ship missiles;

- Provide air control for aircraft;

- Refuel and reprovision escorts; and

- Establish a highly capable and visual naval presence.

One of the first tasks for the modernization program was to change the feed stock for the boilers. The black oil that was used to fire the boilers was changed to naval distillate fuel, which was lighter and stored at a higher natural temperature. This meant that the fuel-oil storage and transfer tanks, 130 in total, had to be cleaned of the asphalt-like residue of the black oil and then coated with an epoxy. In addition, all the pipes used in the fuel piping system were cleaned and modified for use with the new fuel. The fuel tank–heating system for the black oil was no longer needed, and the tank-heating coils and their wiring were removed or closed off.

The other task was to remove all vestiges of the World War II antiaircraft gun system and the four 5-inch gun mounts from the second level of both port and starboard sides, two mounts per side. This was to create space for the installation of armored boxes carrying Tomahawk guided missiles.

Iowa was then towed to Ingalls Shipbuilding in Pascagoula, Mississippi. Over the next several months, the battleship was upgraded with the most advanced weaponry available. Among the new weapons systems were 4 MK 141 quad-cell launchers for 16 AGM-84 Harpoon antiship missiles, 8 armored box-launcher mounts for 32 BGM-109 Tomahawk missiles, which could be nuclear armed, and 4 Phalanx CIWS (close-in weapon system) Gatling guns for defense against enemy antiship missiles and enemy aircraft.

Radar for air search, surface search, and director target search were all upgraded. Air search was upgraded with the SPS-49 set and antenna, surface search with SPS-10, and the director with CIWS VPS-2. The Combat Engagement Center was equipped with the AN/SLQ32 electronic warfare system that brought together all the data produced by these systems to produce a clear picture of the threats to the ship. This allowed the officers manning the warfare system to determine which countermeasures to employ against the threat. An electronic countermeasure component of the system could jam several enemy sensor systems simultaneously. In addition, four Super Rapid Bloom Offboard Countermeasures Chaff and Decoy (SRBOC) launchers were installed to confuse cruise missiles in the terminal phase of their approach.

The Phalanx CIWS searches for and automatically engages missiles and aircraft that have penetrated the longer-range defense systems. The search system for the Phalanx was by AN/VPS-2 pulsed Doppler radar. The Tomahawk and Harpoon missiles were preprogrammed with a range of target data sets. Before launch, target selection was made in the Strike Warfare Center and then transmitted to the missile for programming into the missile's guidance system.

An interesting note is that the modernization program did not need to be adopted for the Mark 8 Ford rangekeeper, notwithstanding its mechanical analog calculating devices including gears, cams, and multipliers. This mechanical system was first trialed as a prototype rangekeeper installed on board USS *Texas* in July 1916. The review to digitally computerize the rangekeeper determined that the effort and cost were not justified when comparing the likely outcome to the accuracy and efficiency of this established historic system. However, the Mark 48 shore-bombardment computer had been built with analog electronic components, and its signals could be integrated with the rangekeeper.

Crew comfort was also addressed by installing seven 125-ton air-conditioning systems. Crew sleeping arrangements were changed from open racks to bunks with mattresses and privacy curtains.

USS *Iowa* was recommissioned on 28 April 1984 at Ingalls Shipbuilding, with Vice President George

(above) An elevated stern view of USS *Iowa* undergoing modernization/reactivation construction at Ingalls Shipbuilding shipyard. (NARA)

(right, top) An elevated starboard bow view of USS *Iowa* undergoing modernization/reactivation construction at Ingalls Shipbuilding shipyard. (NARA)

(right, bottom) A port amidships view of the superstructure on USS *Iowa* during reactivation at Ingalls Shipbuilding. From the left, in green paint, is the mounting structure for whip antennas, the armored conning tower known as Spot 3, and, covered with a tarp, SKY-1, the forward 5-in gun director. (NARA)

UNITED STATES NAVAL INSTITUTE

(above) Two crew members on USS *Iowa* discuss how to move a 16-in projectile. (NARA)

(right, top) The centerline passageway known as Broadway on the third deck of USS *Iowa*. (NARA)

(right, bottom) The port side serving line of the enlisted galley on USS *Iowa*. (NARA)

UNITED STATES NAVAL INSTITUTE

The SPS-49 search radar on USS *Iowa*. (NARA)

H. W. Bush and Secretary of the Navy John Lehman in attendance. Following the completion of her modernization program, the ship sailed to Guantánamo Bay and Puerto Rico for trials of her engines and guns.

With the shakedown cruise completed, the *Iowa* commenced with her "presence" cruises to show U.S. Navy strength in areas where Soviet influence might have been undermining local governments. Upon sailing through the Panama Canal, she cruised along the west coast of Central America, providing humanitarian aid and medical assistance to the local populations of Costa Rica and Honduras. In addition, the *Iowa* carried out surveillance operations off the coast of Nicaragua. Returning to the United States, the ship had a week-long visit in New York during October 1984.

Also in 1984, USS *Iowa* undertook a series of exercises to test the accuracy of her 16-inch gunfire. The exercises had been ordered by Secretary Lehman in the wake of a controversial action in Lebanon in which USS *New Jersey* fired on Syrian army artillery in the mountains overlooking Beirut. While the hostile forces were destroyed by the 16-inch shells, a newspaper reporter claimed that some shells had struck civilian areas. In response, Lehman wished to demonstrate to the world the accuracy and effectiveness of U.S. naval artillery.

To give *Iowa*'s gunnery crew a clear accuracy objective, John Lehman set guidelines that a salvo of 16-inch shells must land within a circle matching the area of the U.S. Capitol building. This caused a substantial reevaluation of the dynamics that went into setting the aiming parameters for the 16-inch guns. A significant component of the firing dynamics was the quality of the stored propellant and its structure within its casing. In addition, Doppler velocimeters were installed on the middle gun to provide measurement of the initial velocity of the shell exiting the gun barrel. By the end of the exercises the guidelines had been achieved, as impressively demonstrated when salvo results were diagrammed and overlaid on a map of the Capitol. USS *Iowa* was famed as the most accurate of naval vessels.

The following year, 1985, the *Iowa* joined her NATO allies to demonstrate her new military capabilities in Russia's front yard. First she sailed into the Arctic Circle over the route that Russian submarines and surface ships would sail to enter the Atlantic. The NATO ships and *Iowa* sailed under complete electronic silence to avoid both radio and radar emissions that could be captured by Russian early warning systems. This also provided an opportunity to test her 1940s capabilities by using her optical fire-control system. She fired her 16-inch guns at an iceberg and landed six 16-inch rounds on her frozen target at 12,000 yards.

(right, top) Guests take their seats at dockside for recommissioning of USS *Iowa*. (NARA)

(below) A Marine color guard renders honors on board USS *Iowa* during the ship's recommissioning. (NARA)

(right, middle) Secretary of the Navy John F. Lehman speaks during the recommissioning of USS *Iowa*. (NARA)

(far right bottom) Vice President George H. W. Bush arrives aboard USS *Iowa* for the ship's recommissioning. (NARA)

A round is fired from the No. 3 Mark 7 16-in/50-cal gun turret during gunnery exercises on USS *Iowa*. The barrel is elevated to the 03 level to test the effects of 16-in gun overpressure on the Tomahawk armored box launcher located on that level. (NARA)

A 2,700-pound projectile is fired from the barrel of a forward 16-in gun on USS *Iowa* during sea trials off the coast of Mississippi. The battleship was scheduled to be recommissioned into the Fleet on 28 April 1984, after completion of modernization/reactivation construction at Ingalls Shipbuilding, Pascagoula, Mississippi. (NARA)

USS IOWA (BB-61) 16 INCH FIRINGS
21 JULY 1984

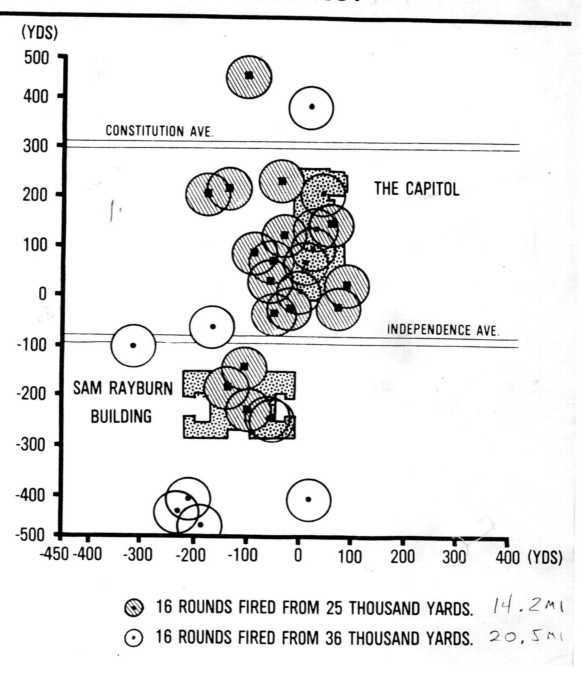

16 ROUNDS FIRED FROM 25 THOUSAND YARDS. *14.2 MI*

16 ROUNDS FIRED FROM 36 THOUSAND YARDS. *20.5 MI*

Salvo results for the *Iowa*'s 16-in guns from 25,000 and 36,000 yards (14.2 and 20.5 miles, respectively), diagrammed as if the U.S. Capitol and the Sam Rayburn Office Building had been the targets. (NARA)

(left) Crew members monitor radar screens in the combat information center on USS *Iowa*. (NARA)

(below) Waves crash on the bow of USS *Iowa* while under way in rough seas. The ship is participating in NATO exercise Ocean Safari '85. (NARA)

Then the *Iowa* sailed into the Baltic. She visited Oslo, Norway, and paid courtesy calls at Copenhagen in Denmark and Kiel in Germany to show her NATO allies and the public her capabilities to protect them from Russian aggression. The *Iowa*'s presence in the Baltic was a clear message to the Russians that the U.S. Navy had a right and ability to sail anywhere in international waters that lapped Russian coasts. After port calls, the *Iowa* undertook exercises with NATO ships on antisubmarine drills, using the new Sikorsky Seahawk helicopter. After sailing the Arctic and Baltic waters, *Iowa* returned to Norfolk and then headed again to the Caribbean and Central America as part of her "presence" role.

On the Fourth of July in 1986, *Iowa* carried President Ronald Reagan for the International Naval Review on the Hudson River in New York. Operational and training exercises of Florida's east and west coasts followed during early August. On 2 August *Iowa* launched a Tomahawk missile on the Eglin Air Force Base range in the Florida Panhandle. *Iowa* participated in NATO exercises off Norway in September, with port visits to Portsmouth in England and Bremerhaven in West Germany.

On her return to Norfolk in October, *Iowa* conducted sea trials off the Virginia Capes. The ship undertook the first battleship launch of a Pioneer remotely piloted vehicle (RPV), intended for use in fire-control by

The port 01 level superstructure of USS *Iowa*. (NARA)

transmitting video of the fall of shot from the ship's 16-inch guns. The Pioneer was successfully launched and then was controlled to return to the ship and land in a safety barrier on the ship's aft deck. *Iowa*'s successful launch and recovery led to the installation of Pioneer vehicles on all four *Iowa*-class battleships.

The use of the Pioneer drone was more than fire control. During Desert Storm, the operation to liberate Kuwait from Iraqi forces, USS *Wisconsin* took the surrender of Iraqi troops who signaled their surrender to the ship's drone rather than suffer another bombardment of 16-inch shells.

The RPV, which carries a stabilized television camera and a laser designator, was tested on board the *Iowa* as a basic gunfire support system with over-the-horizon targeting and reconnaissance capabilities. The system may be operated out to a range of 110 miles from the battleship surface group and has an endurance of eight hours.

A crew member monitors the SPS-49 radar screen on USS *Iowa*. (NARA)

Crew from USS *Iowa*, foreground, and the frigate USS *Trippe* (FF-1075) fall into ranks prior to manning replenishment stations. (NARA)

USS *Iowa* fires its Mark 7 16-in/50-cal guns during NATO exercise BALTOPS '85. (NARA)

A port bow view of USS *Iowa* moored to a pier at Akershus Castle, Oslo, Norway. (NARA)

A sailor cleans a piece of equipment in the magazine of one of the Mark 7 16-in/50-cal gun turrets on USS *Iowa*. (NARA)

USS *Iowa* receives fuel from the fleet oiler USS *Merrimack* (AO 179) during an underway replenishment. (NARA)

Crew members stand by for instructions on the deck of USS *Iowa* during an underway replenishment with NATO exercise ships during exercise Northern Wedding '86 in the North Atlantic Ocean. (NARA)

Crew members on board USS *Iowa* participate in an underway replenishment from an oiler during NATO exercise Northern Wedding '86 in the North Atlantic Ocean. (NARA)

In September 1987 USS *Iowa* sailed from Norfolk to the Mediterranean to join the Sixth Fleet and take part in the exercise Display Determination. This monthlong NATO exercise had ships from the United States, the United Kingdom, Italy, Turkey, Portugal, France, and the Netherlands working together, with the USS *Saratoga* as flagship. During the exercise, the cruise ship *Achille Lauro* was captured by Palestinian terrorists and a passenger was killed. The terrorists were allowed to board a passenger jet in Egypt, but President Reagan had the *Saratoga* launch F-14 Tomcat fighters to intercept the jet and force it to land in Italy, where the terrorists were arrested.

Following a port visit to Istanbul on 8 October, the *Iowa* detached from the Sixth Fleet and sailed to the North Sea for additional NATO exercises off Norway, with a port visit to Trondheim on 30 October. She then sailed back to the Mediterranean, through the Suez Canal on 25 November, and on to Diego Garcia, a U.S. and British military base in the Indian Ocean. From this location *Iowa* conducted operations in the Indian Ocean and Arabian Sea and escorted convoys through the Strait of Hormuz during the "tanker war" with Iran. Duties included protecting the convoy assembly areas off

(top) Crew members of USS *Iowa* participate in an underway replenishment operation with the ammunition ship USS *Nitro* (AE 23) during NATO exercise Northern Wedding '86 in the North Atlantic Ocean. (NARA)

(middle) A crew member monitors the SLQ-32 radar warning system console on p USS *Iowa*. (NARA)

(bottom) An elevated port bow view of USS *Iowa* as it refuels the guided-missile destroyer USS *Halyburton* (FFG-40) during an underway replenishment. The ships are participating in NATO exercise Ocean Safari '85. (NARA)

Masirah Island and Muscat, which lasted for the month of January 1988 and well into February. She sailed back through the Suez Canal and into the Mediterranean on 20 February, then back to Norfolk. *Iowa* departed Norfolk to participate in New York's Fleet Week, 21–25 April. For the balance of April and into August, *Iowa* was in Norfolk at the Naval Shipyard for repair and maintenance.

Following sea trials off the Virginia Capes in August, *Iowa* sailed to Port Everglades and then on to Guantánamo Bay. She arrived on 13 October for refresher training prior to gunnery exercises at Vieques Island, Puerto Rico. *Iowa* returned to Norfolk on 7 December 1988. In the new year she sailed back to the Caribbean to visit Saint Martin with the standing U.S. Naval forces in the Atlantic. During this exercise she undertook further gunnery trials at Vieques Island and fired her 16-inch guns at 23.4 nautical miles, the longest recorded range of any battleship. This was followed on 5 February by a five-day port visit to New Orleans for the Mardi Gras celebrations, with active participation by officers and crew members.

USS *Iowa* returned to Norfolk for repairs to fuel lines damaged during an exercise. On 29 March officers, chiefs, and petty officers, with other battleship sailors and technicians from ordnance facilities, attended a conference on gunnery improvements. On 13 April *Iowa* departed Norfolk for the Caribbean and further gunnery exercises as part of Fleet Exercise 3-89.

(top) Visitors tour USS *Iowa* while the ship is in Portsmouth Harbour, England. (NARA)

(middle) USS *Iowa* launches a Harpoon antiship cruise missile during Fleet Exercise 2-86. (NARA)

(bottom) PCC William Sanders sorts mail bags on USS *Iowa*. (NARA)

A starboard bow view of USS *Iowa*. (NARA)

A Pioneer I remotely piloted vehicle (RPV) is launched during a rocket booster-assisted takeoff from the stern of USS *Iowa*. (NARA)

Crew members work in the Combat Information Center on USS *Iowa*. (NARA)

A Pioneer I remotely piloted vehicle (RPV) approaches a recovery net erected on the stern of USS *Iowa*. (NARA)

A bow view of USS *Iowa* under way. (NARA)

A gunner's mate loads ammunition into the Phalanx Mark 15 close-in weapons system on USS *Iowa*. (NARA)

Marine CAPT Richard D. Benjamin mans SKY-1, the forward 5-in gun director on USS *Iowa*. (NARA)

(below) USS *Iowa* fires the center Mark 7 16-in/50-cal gun in the No. 2 turret. The projectile is the 1,000th round fired by the *Iowa*'s 16-in guns since the ship was recommissioned. (NARA)

A port beam view of USS *Iowa* under way off the coast of Lebanon. (NARA)

Combat Information Center on USS *Iowa*. (NARA)

A view of a conical monopole high-frequency antenna mounted on the bow of USS *Iowa*. (NARA)

(below) The No. 2 and No. 3 Mark 7 16-in/50-cal gun turrets of USS *Iowa* are fired to starboard during a main battery gunnery exercise. (NARA)

(above) USS *Iowa* arrives in Newport for repairs. (NARA)

(below) USS *Iowa* is guided into Dry Dock No. 4 at Norfolk Navy Yard. (NARA)

UNITED STATES NAVAL INSTITUTE

SAILING INTO TRAGEDY

The USS *Iowa* was sailing approximately 330 nautical miles northeast of Puerto Rico on 19 April 1989 when she sailed into a tragedy. The subsequent controversy culminated in January 1991 with a recommendation from the General Accounting Office (GAO) that all *Iowa*-class battleships be decommissioned.

At 0953 the center 16-inch gun of turret 2 on board the *Iowa* blew up. The explosion emanated from nearly 500 pounds of D846 propellant behind a 2,700-pound dummy projectile in the gun's open breech. The explosion generated a fireball with a temperature between 2,500 degrees and 3,000 degrees Fahrenheit moving at 2,000 feet per second with a pressure of 4,000 pounds per square inch. This force blew out the door to the gun captains' area and warped the dividing bulkhead. The blast ruptured armored steel bulkheads separating the center gun from its left and right gun neighbors. The explosion of fire and deadly clouds of gas blasted its way downward below the turret house to the electrical and projectile decks and then into the lowest level deck, where the powder-handling room was located. The powder hoist shaft provided a direct link from the turret to the powder-handling room, which was distended by the pressure wave, with the door at the bottom of the hoist failing because of the pressure from the explosion. The fire ignited 25 bags of propellant that had been passed from the magazine through the annular space into the powder-handling room in preparation for hoisting to the gun house.

The crew in the magazine and annular space survived the explosion, as did the USS *Iowa*, but 47 crew members inside turret 2 and its supporting barbette structure tragically did not.

The annular space created by two circular armored bulkheads had provided a flameproof barrier between the turret's powder hoists and the powder-handling room, on one hand, and the magazine, on the other. The annular-space design originated with USS *North Carolina* in 1937 after a 16-year hiatus in U.S. battleship design and was then carried forward with all subsequent U.S. battleships. Previously, the magazine in a U.S. battleship was separated from the powder-handling room by a bulkhead with a door and scuttles opening through it. This was similar to the system used in World War I Royal Navy battlecruisers. The tragic fate of the battlecruiser HMS *Invincible* proved the design disastrously inadequate for preventing flame and flash from an explosion in the turret from reaching the powder stored in the magazine. During the Battle of Jutland, *Invincible* blew up and sank, killing all the crew but six. *Iowa*'s annular space insulated it and its crew from a similar catastrophe.

However, *Iowa* did suffer significant damage from the explosion, with the continuing danger of further damage and deaths until the fires were extinguished. The crew immediately took up firefighting equipment to spray water on the outside of turret 2. On opening the turret 2 escape hatch, a fireman equipped with breathing apparatus and a Kevlar suit entered the turret to start dousing the multiple fires. Other crew members worked their way down through the ship to enter the magazine and annular space and then open a watertight door to the powder-handling room. The handling room contained a mass of twisted bodies, without survivors. However, slowly burning powder bags were still emitting poisonous gas. As nothing more could be done, the door was resealed and orders given to flood the magazine, annular space, and powder-handling room.

Multiple acts of heroism occurred as the *Iowa* crew fought to save fellow crew members and the ship. During the course of the day and evening, bodies and body parts were retrieved from turret 2 and the barbette and were placed in body bags for removal to Dover Air Force Base, Delaware, for postmortem examination.

USS *Iowa* returned to Norfolk in the late afternoon of 23 April. At 0900 the next day a memorial service for the 47 sailors killed on board USS *Iowa* was held in a large Navy Yard hangar. In attendance were President George H. W. Bush and Mrs. Bush, with family members of the deceased and the crew of USS *Iowa*.

To safeguard the operation of the four *Iowa*-class battleships, the Navy had to determine what had caused the explosion in turret 2. The investigation became a controversy as it focused on a single sailor who allegedly placed an incendiary device among the powder bags being loaded into the central gun, thereby setting off the explosion. Uneasy with the Navy's investigation, congressional committees called for further investigation. The GAO asked the Department of Energy's Sandia National Laboratories to review the Navy's technical analysis.

The moment tragedy strikes. A photo taken from the bridge captures the explosion of the No. 2 16-in gun turret on USS *Iowa*. The blast, which occurred as the *Iowa* was conducting routine gunnery exercises 330 miles northeast of Puerto Rico, killed 47 sailors. (NARA)

A photo taken from the bridge captures the explosion of the No. 2 16-in gun turret on USS *Iowa*. (NARA)

A photo taken from the bridge captures the efforts of the crew to combat fire directly after the No. 2 16-in gun turret on USS *Iowa* exploded. (NARA)

The Sandia review neither confirmed nor denied the Navy's conclusion that a deliberate act by a crew member caused the explosion. However, Sandia identified a plausible alternative explanation: a high-speed overram of a propellant bag against the base of a projectile can fracture pellets in the bag's top layer, releasing burning particles that could ignite the black powder in an adjacent powder bag. If that had occurred, it could then have ignited the whole charge and caused the *Iowa*'s explosion.

The Navy accepted the broad thrust of the Sandia report and apologized to the family of the single sailor who had been identified as causing the explosion, as there was no real evidence to support the claim that he had intentionally killed the other sailors.

The GAO report *Issues Arising from the Explosion Aboard the USS Iowa*, published in January 1991, provided a comprehensive analysis of the operation of the ship. It identified a broad range of factors that could have contributed to the explosion. Chief among these was the undermanning of the ship, the lack of hands-on training for the crew in operating the 16-inch guns, and conducting unauthorized gunnery shoots.

During the review and controversy, the *Iowa* sailed for Europe on 7 June 1989. It paid a port visit to Kiel, sailed into and out of the Baltic, and paid port visits also to Portsmouth, England, and Rota, Spain. She then headed into the Mediterranean, putting into port at Marseilles, France, for repair and maintenance. On 2 August *Iowa* undertook four days of gunnery

Sailors line the rails and Marines stand at attention beneath the No. 2 16-in gun turret of the USS *Iowa* as the battleship comes home four days after an explosion in the No. 2 killed 47 of its crew. (NARA)

exercises with turrets 1 and 3. Turret 2 had been locked and trained to point forward and was inoperative. Following the successful firing of her 16-inch guns, *Iowa* sailed to the coast of Lebanon in support of the U.S. Embassy, which was under siege by a Lebanese Maronite militia. Embassy staff were rescued by helicopter, and the *Iowa* sailed for Gaeta, Italy, to continue her Mediterranean mission of showing the strength and mobility of the U.S. Navy. She made port visits to Casablanca, Morocco; Gibraltar; Antalya and Istanbul, Turkey; Haifa, Israel; Alexandria, Egypt;

Ajaccio, Corsica; Augusta Bay, Sicily; Naples, Italy; and Palma, Mallorca.

Iowa then sailed for Norfolk. In transit, she fired for the last time a 16-inch shell from her guns, totaling 11,834 rounds fired since her 1943 commissioning and 2,873 shells fired since her recommissioning in 1984. *Iowa* entered Norfolk Navy Yard on 7 December 1989. A memorial plaque for turret 2 was unveiled on 4 January 1990 and dedicated on 19 April at a service on the one-year anniversary of the tragedy. The *Iowa* was decommissioned on 26 October 1990.

Mark 36 rapid bloom offboard countermeasures launchers on USS *Iowa*. They are used as defensive weapons against incoming heat-seeking missiles. (NARA)

Under way in formation off the coast of Lebanon are, from left, the guided-missile cruiser USS *Belknap* (CG-26), USS *Iowa*, the aircraft carrier USS *Coral Sea* (CV-43), and the amphibious assault ship USS *Nassau* (LHA-4). (NARA)

USS *Iowa* is welcomed and escorted by small boats as she passes Victorian Fort guarding entrance to Portsmouth Harbour, England. (NARA)

A NEW FUTURE FOR USS *IOWA*

This magnificent ship, USS *Iowa*, is a testimony to the skills of U.S. Navy ship designers, the shipbuilding skills of the Brooklyn Navy Yard, the inventive and technological abilities of U.S. industry, and the professional and heroic skills of the U.S. sailors who stayed on duty against multiple enemies over decades of operational experience. When tragedy struck, *Iowa* heroes jumped forward and ran the decks to rescue colleagues and preserve the ship.

The *Iowa* earned nine battle stars during her operations in the Pacific in World War II and two additional battle stars from her Korean War service. Her service from April 1984 until October 1990 coincided with confrontation with the Soviet Union. Parading with purpose off the coast of Soviet Russia and in the Baltic Sea, the Black Sea, and the Sea of Okhotsk, the *Iowa* and her sister *Iowa*-class battleships demonstrated the global mobility and reach of the U.S. Navy. The Soviet Union dissolved itself in December 1991.

The decommissioned *Iowa* was stored initially at the Philadelphia Naval Shipyard and then moved to join the Reserve Fleet in Suisun Bay, near San Francisco, on 21 April 2001. In 2006 the National Defense Authorization Act authorized the Navy to remove the *Iowa* from the Naval Vessel Register and offer the ship for donation to an eligible entity that would display the ship in California.

Following an evaluation of competing claims, the Navy selected the Pacific Battleship Center as the successful recipient of the *Iowa* on 6 September 2011. On 19 June 2012 the *Iowa* was anchored at Berth 87, San Pedro waters, Port of Los Angeles, California—the original anchorage for the U.S. Pacific Fleet. The *Iowa* opened as a museum and visitor center.

The *Iowa* hosts 420,000 visitors a year and provides science, technology, engineering, and math education facilities for 20,000 students within the Los Angeles area. The ship is supported by 350,000 volunteer hours that help restore and maintain it. Many of the volunteers are veterans and are themselves supported by American Legion Post #61.

The *Iowa* is close to the naval base in San Diego, which is home to the Naval Surface Force. The

This fleet of small craft transported signatories to the Surrender Instrument aboard the USS *Missouri* for the historic ceremony on 2 September, 1945. On the horizon is the USS *Iowa*. (U.S. Naval Institute photo archive)

commander of this force uses the *Iowa* to host Basic Division Officer courses and Chief Petty Officer courses on naval history and heritage of the surface navy.

An important and new development for the *Iowa* is her selection to become the home for the National Museum of the Surface Navy. The Pacific Battleship Center secured the rights to build the Surface Navy Museum through a licensing agreement with the U.S. Navy in 2018 and a congressional designation in 2021. The Freedom of the Seas campaign to build the museum is guided by the vision to "inspire global awareness of freedom of the seas," and the campaign's mission is to "ignite curiosity, connect communities, and enhance understanding of America's role in maritime peace and prosperity."

Over the next ten years the three-phase plan starts with a planned move to the anchor location in the Old Fishing Slip for a redeveloped San Pedro Public Market on the LA Waterfront. A veteran's park and large amphitheater will be built adjacent to the ship. On board the *Iowa*, 15,000 square feet of extra exhibit space will be cleared by removing berthing spaces.

Plus, approximately 20,000 square feet of below-deck exhibit space is planned as well as a building ashore that will provide an additional 20,000 to 50,000 square feet.

The timeline to build the museum pending donations and financial support is

- [2025] Phase 1: Core Experience on board Battleship *Iowa*

- [2028] Phase 2: Expanded Experience on board Battleship *Iowa*

- [2030] Phase 3: Freedom of the Seas Park and Pavilion

- [2034] Phase 4: Deep-Dive Experience on board Battleship *Iowa*

This exciting development will mean that many more Americans will be able to appreciate the inherent power of Battleship *Iowa* and how she helped maintain and safeguard the freedom and democracy of the United States.

NATIONAL MUSEUM OF THE
SURFACE NAVY AT THE BATTLESHIP *IOWA*

Picture this: it's 2010 and the final battleship in the United States Navy is languishing in the obscurity of the Suisun Bay Reserve Fleet. She's a legend, but she's the only remaining ship of her class that has yet to become a museum. The possibility of her being broken up looms ever darker on her horizon.

Enter the Pacific Battleship Center (PBC), a passionate non-profit determined to save the world's last battleship. On September 6, 2011, after negotiating the Navy's complicated donation process, they were awarded custody of BB-61, the retired USS *Iowa*.

This barely scratches the surface of a difficult and far more involved process and was merely the prelude of *Iowa*'s epic story. Bringing *Iowa* to her present location on the main channel of the busiest port complex in the western hemisphere required gaining the trust of the U.S. Navy; three million dollars of appropriation funding from the State of Iowa; public hearings and

garnering community support in the City and Port of Los Angeles; months of restoration work at a dock in Richmond, CA; a days-long ocean tow from San Francisco; donations of time, labor, and funds from motivated Americans; and intense amounts of blood, sweat, tears, grit, and vision.

All those elements came together on July 6, 2012, when *Iowa* opened to the public as the west coast's only battleship museum.

She's on a new mission now: bridging the past and present to shape the future. To ensure *Iowa* stays relevant to society, her current crew has developed a world-class experience that inspires visitors of all ages. Fascinating tours and public programs bring the ship to life for new generations. These offerings combined with a friendly, family atmosphere quickly propelled her to her current ranking as the #4 museum and attraction in Los Angeles.

The education team creates real-world correlations with STEM (Science Technology Engineering Math) and history—including an overnight stay that sparks the imagination. The military and veterans department provides service members of all branches assistance and a sense of camaraderie. The ship has become an integral part of her community, offering not only free events for locals, but acting as a training hub for first responders, disaster planners, and members of the military.

To foster connection between civilians and the nation's armed forces, the PBC team co-founded LA Fleet Week with the City and Port of Los Angeles in 2016. The objective—to transform public perception of the Navy and its mission—is achieved by hosting a festival adjacent to *Iowa* over Memorial Day weekend. Featuring Navy ships, military aircraft and equipment, food vendors, exhibits, competitions, bands, and more, LA Fleet Week is a catalyst for the local economy, drawing around 100,000 visitors and generating millions of dollars in revenue annually for local restaurants and businesses.

In 2018 PBC's leadership learned of an initiative to create a national museum for the US Navy's surface forces. Understanding the opportunity this project presented, they jumped at the chance to take on a new challenge.

Scheduled to open in 2025 in conjunction with the Navy's 250th birthday, the National Museum of the Surface Navy will introduce immersive, interactive experiences unlike any seen before. The museum, housed in existing spaces aboard Battleship *Iowa*, will raise America's awareness of the importance of the

United States Surface Naval Forces' role in "freedom of the seas"—the right of all to free and open access to the world's waterways.

Thanks to a 2022 award of $6.7 million dollars from the State of California, PBC will construct the Freedom of the Seas Park and Pavilion, a 17,500 square foot multi-purpose community center and events space. In addition to hosting community events, it will be home to the Freedom of the Seas Awards.

These awards were established in 2021 to honor those that embody the core principles of America's

Surface Navy: to protect and defend our oceans for the benefit of the free world. They are presented yearly on the anniversary of the Battle of Leyte Gulf to deserving recipients who display extraordinary commitment to concepts such as leadership, humanitarian service, enhancing commerce and communication, furthering innovation and exploration, and embodying the Navy's core principles: international relations, free trade, humanitarian assistance, and technological innovation.

As it moves forward, the National Museum of the Surface Navy at the Battleship *Iowa* looks to ignite curiosity, connect communities, and enhance understanding of America's role in maritime peace and prosperity, and for honoring the service of Surface Navy sailors since 1775.

World of Warships is a free-to-play, naval warfare-themed, massively multiplayer online game produced and published by Wargaming. Like their other games, *World of Tanks* (WoT) and *World of Warplanes* (WoWP), players take control of historic vehicles to battle others in player-vs-player battles or play cooperatively against bots in a player-versus-environment (PvE) mode. *World of Warships* (WoWs) was originally released for on PC in 2015 and was followed in 2018 by a mobile adaptation, *World of Warships Blitz*. The PlayStation 4 and Xbox One console version, titled *World of Warships: Legends*, released in 2019 and became available on PlayStation 5 and Xbox Series X/S in April 2021.

Developed by Wargaming d.o.o. in Belgrade, Serbia, *World of Warships* (PC) currently has millions of registered players – playing on four main servers across the globe. More than 500 dedicated staff members work on a four-week update cycle to bring new features, ships, and mechanics to the game – keeping gameplay fresh and inviting to new players. The game features more than 700 ships, spread across 13 different in-game nations. Ships are designed based on historical documents and actual blueprints from the first half of the 20th century, and it takes from two to six months on average to create each of these ships. There are more than 23 ports to choose from, and 16 of them are re-created based on historic harbors and port towns.

There are five different ship classes—destroyers, cruisers, battleships, aircraft carriers, and submarines—with each class offering a different gameplay experience. Ships are arranged in tiers between I and X, plus so-called superships, which represent the pinnacle of naval engineering from World War II and the early Cold War era. Players must progress through ship classes and tiers to reach tier X, after which they get access to these behemoths. Each warship needs a naval commander to lead it into battle, and there are many commanders to choose from in *World of Warships*, including more than 15 iconic historical figures. In *World of Warships*, players can battle on more than 40 maps. There are seven different permanent or seasonal Battle Types to choose from, including Co-op Battles, Random Battles, Ranked Battles, Clan Battles, Brawls, and Scenarios. From time to time, additional special Event battles are held.

USS *Iowa* is proudly represented in *World of Warships* at tier IX, available to research in the Fast Battleships branch of the U.S. Navy tech tree. The legendary ship is also present in *World of Warships: Legends* and *World of Warships Blitz* at tiers VII and IX, respectively. Will you take the reins of America's most powerful battleship? Try her out in *World of Warships* today!

Developed by the team behind *World of Warships* for PC, *World of Warships: Legends* is a different entry in Wargaming's flagship nautical franchise that takes full advantage of the power and capabilities of home consoles. *World of Warships: Legends* brings the online naval action loved by millions to home consoles for the very first time, alongside a host of content and features exclusive to the console experience. *World of Warships: Legends* is now available to download from the PlayStation® Store and Microsoft Store. Players can now wage wars across a variety of maps, in numerous warships, and enjoy stunning oceanic vistas with glorious HDR support on PlayStation®4 and Xbox One X. Full 4K support is available on PlayStation®4 Pro and PlayStation®5, and Xbox One X too! and *Legends* also supports standard high-def on PlayStation®4 and Xbox One, with more intriguing graphics on the horizon.

Wargaming proudly supports various charitable causes that members of the gaming and history community deeply care for:

Supporting veterans and servicemembers

- Operation Lifeboat (2020) raised $150,000 USD for Stack Up's mental health awareness helpline

- Remembrance charity drive (2020) raised $45,000 USD for Help for Heroes, which supports UK veterans and service members

- Project Valor (2017) saw *WoWS*, *WoT*, and *WoWP* raising $75,000 USD for a veteran housing program

BALDT ANCHOR

Patented in 1898 by American engineer Frederick Baldt, it was adopted as the standard anchor design of the U.S. Navy in the early 20th century. To this day, it is still the primary anchor design of the Navy.

Stockless anchors—as seen here—were originally patented in the U.K. in 1821, allowing the anchor to pulled into a ship's Hawsehole. The *Iowa*-class battleships had two 30,000lb anchors each, the chains supporting them were made of links that weighed over 128 lbs each.

World of Warships partners with museums across the world to support the preservation of naval history and the education of the global community.

In celebration of 2021's International Museum Day, Wargaming, in partnership with Verizon, organized The Longest Night of Museums livestream. The online event included free virtual tours of 15 different naval museums worldwide, attracting million viewers on Twitch alone.

In July 2021 Wargaming partnered with Imperial War Museum to launch an interactive gaming room atop London's iconic museum ship HMS *Belfast*.

- $50,000 USD raised for the restoration of USS *Batfish*, *Muskogee* (2019)

- $400,000 USD raised for the restoration of USS *Texas*, *Houston* (since 2017)

- $20,000 USD raised in partnership with the French-speaking community for the restoration of the submarine *Espadon* (2021)

- $50,000 USD raised for the Nauticus museum to restore one of the main turrets of USS *Wisconsin*. (2024)

WORKING UNIFORM

Shown: Signal Officers communicating with a signal light.

In accordance with U.S. Navy uniform regulations, when a ship was at anchor, the crew could only appear on the upper deck wearing an undress service uniform. When working in the engine room, gun turrets, and other internal compartments, personnel had to wear a light blue cotton shirt, and dark blue canvas trousers—similar to blue jeans today. However, navy sailors began to adopt this uniform as their daily working attire in all situations—including in combat. This attire was favored due to being comfortable, loose fitting and breathable, as well as including plenty of pockets and a sturdy work belt. The uniform was typically topped with a white "dixie cup" cap titled over the back of the head.